IMAGES
*of America*

# THE KNICKERBOCKER
# SNOWSTORM

Pictured is the 600 block of Pennsylvania Avenue during the Knickerbocker Snowstorm on January 28, 1922. The record-setting snow accumulated 28 inches at Twenty-fourth and M Streets NW. (The Historical Society of Washington, DC.)

ON THE COVER: This is a wide view of the police lines and snow-covered streets that surround the Knickerbocker Theater as hundreds of spectators watch the rescue effort on January 29, 1922. The theater roof, weighed down by snow, collapsed on the evening of January 28 during a silent picture show. The theater was located at Eighteenth Street and Columbia Road NW. (Cezar Del Valle.)

IMAGES
*of America*

# THE KNICKERBOCKER
# SNOWSTORM

Kevin Ambrose

ARCADIA
PUBLISHING

Published by Arcadia Publishing
Charleston, South Carolina


Library of Congress Control Number: 2012942485

For all general information, please contact Arcadia Publishing:
Telephone 843-853-2070
Fax 843-853-0044
E-mail sales@arcadiapublishing.com
For customer service and orders:
Toll-Free 1-888-313-2665

Visit us on the Internet at www.arcadiapublishing.com

*This book is dedicated to the victims of the Knickerbocker
Theater Disaster. Their story lives on.*

# CONTENTS

# ACKNOWLEDGMENTS

In assembling and organizing the photographs and text for this book, I received invaluable assistance from a number of organizations and individuals. Organizations include: the Library of Congress; the Historical Society of Washington, DC; the Alexandria Library Special Collections; the Jewish Historical Society of Greater Washington; the Martin Luther King Jr. Memorial Library; the Kiplinger Research Library; the NOAA Central Library; Congressional Cemetery; the United States Park Police; the *Washington Post*; the *Alexandria Times*; the Associated Press; *Weatherwise* magazine; Ancestry.com; and the Capital Weather Gang. Individuals who helped with is effort include: Jason Samenow, Ian Livingston, Andy Weiss, Dan Henry, Adam Lewis, , John Madert, Kathy Baker, Nick Barkas, Frank Lyman, Debbie Chambers, Marge Miller, Christen Runge, Lisa Edkins, Julie Downie, Robin Nordlinger Leiman, Clair Uziel, Barry Reichenbaugh, Cezar Del Valle, Don Sutherland, Paul Williams, and Jim Walline. If any organization or individual has been omitted from this list, the oversight is unintentional.

While a bibliography is not included in this effort, the following books provided helpful information: *Capital Losses* by James Goode; *Lost Washington, DC* by John DeFerrari; *Washington Weather* by Kevin Ambrose, Dan Henry, and Andy Weiss; *Blizzards and Snowstorms of Washington, DC* by Kevin Ambrose; *Snowmageddon* by Kevin Ambrose and Ian Livingston; *General Patton* by Stanley P. Hirshson; and *The Button Box* by Ruth Ellen Patton Totten.

# INTRODUCTION

In the recorded history of Washington, DC, the Knickerbocker storm remains unsurpassed, both for the amount of snow it produced and for its devastating toll on human life.

The collapse of the roof at the Knickerbocker Theater, which took 98 lives (many of them children), was described by the *Washington Post* as recently as January 2000 as "the greatest disaster in Washington history."

The horror of what transpired is captured in this excerpt from the *Washington Post*, originally published January 29, 1928, and reprinted January 29, 2000:

> An eye witness to the catastrophe, a man who had just entered the theater and who barely escaped with his life, said that a hearty peal of laughter preceded the falling of the roof. "Great God!" he exclaimed. "It was the most heart-rending thing I ever want to witness." In the lobby of the theater, firemen and policemen and strong civilians worked as best they could in an endeavor to extricate the wounded and the dead. It was a task that tried the souls of men. When the crash first came, it was followed by the screams of women and the shouts of men. Agonizing cries pierced the air. One woman, in particular, shouted at the top of her voice—shouted not for help, or aid, or succor; because she was probably not conscious of what happened. Her shouts were the gasps of the dying, and doctors said so. One mighty symposium of exquisite pain had voiced a united appeal for help, or relief, when all of a sudden there was silence. Those who shouted were those who were under the weight of a roof and a balcony. And what a weight. What a tangled mass. Standing there in the doorways that led to the lobby, the usually stoic policemen almost despaired. The firemen, whose ordinary task is to combat fallen structures, find their way among debris, were appalled. They seemed hopeless in the face of this duty; but they all went to work with a determination of giving every help that was in the power of mortal man.

The storm itself was remarkable for its persevering intensity, generating snowfall rates of greater than one inch per hour over the 24-hour period from Friday afternoon January 27 to Saturday afternoon January 28. Twenty-five inches fell in that span, establishing a 24-hour snowfall record.

All told, the storm laid down 28 inches of snow, more than any other storm in more than 130 years of official Washington, DC, weather records. Subfreezing temperatures in the days preceding the storm meant every flake stuck—an important factor in the catastrophic collapse of the roof of the Knickerbocker Theater.

The cold weather had become established by a blocking pattern, common prior to and during great District of Columbia snowstorms. In such a pattern, a traffic jam of sorts sets up in atmosphere. High pressure over Greenland backs the flow in the atmosphere resulting in a large dip in the jet stream over eastern North America. The dip in the jet stream allows Arctic air to plunge south into the Mid-Atlantic states.

Under these circumstances, storminess can develop along the periphery of the cold air mass, where it collides with mild, moist air, often along the southeast coast of the United States.

In the history of the District of Columbia's great snow events, the Knickerbocker storm evolved in classic form. It originated from a developing area of low pressure off the Georgia coast that crawled northeastward, gaining strength from the steepening contrast between a massive area of bitter, dry Arctic air over the Street Lawrence Valley and mild, moist Atlantic air over the Gulf Stream. But unlike some of the District of Columbia's big snowstorms, it did not charge up the coast like a traditional nor'easter. Rather, once the storm reached the latitude of Cape Hatteras, North Carolina, it slid east-northeast out to sea. As a result, locations to the north received much less snow. New York City, for example, only logged seven inches.

The storm's gradual intensification and increasing distance from the coast spared the region from battering winds but allowed temperatures to moderate to around freezing as the storm departed. The snow's consistency transformed from powdery to heavy and wet, adding to the burden on the roof of the Knickerbocker Theater, which proved too much.

The storm not only led to the trauma at the Knickerbocker Theater but also paralyzed the entire city. Consider this excerpt from a report out of *Weatherwise* magazine: "The city was from the standpoint of transportation, isolated and helpless. Street cars were no longer operating, and it was stated that nine trains were stalled on the tracks between Washington and nearby Alexandria, Virginia."

Perhaps the most analogous storm to the Knickerbocker in more recent times was the "Snowmageddon" storm of February 4–6, 2010, which produced 18 to 32 inches of snow across the DC area. Reagan National Airport—Washington, DC's official measurement site—received 17.8 inches. Although that is some 10 inches less than the Knickerbocker storm, measurements from the Knickerbocker storm were taken at Twenty-fourth and M Streets NW in the district, preventing a direct comparison.

Like the Knickerbocker storm, the Snowmageddon storm was not a traditional East Coast "bomb" that rapidly intensified and raked the entire East Coast. Rather, it was slow-moving, moisture-laden storm that drifted away from the Mid-Atlantic coast, sparing New England.

—Jason Samenow
Weather Editor, the *Washington Post*

# One

# RECORD-BREAKING SNOWSTORM

Exactly 150 years after the Washington and Jefferson Snowstorm of 1772 buried the region under three feet of snow, Washington's largest snowstorm of the century started during the late afternoon of January 27, 1922. By 8:00 a.m. the following morning, the snow had reached 18 inches, breaking the previous 24-hour snowfall record of 12 inches.

By mid-afternoon, the accumulation reached a depth of 25 inches. The snow did not stop until early on the morning of January 29, when it reached 28 inches, an official measurement recorded at Twenty-fourth and M Streets NW. This is a single storm snowfall record for Washington, DC, that still stands today. A snow depth of 33 inches was measured in nearby Rock Creek Park. Temperatures were in the 20s during most of the storm but rose slowly toward the freezing mark as the precipitation ended. The liquid equivalent of the snowfall was an impressive 3.02 inches.

The storm responsible for the record snowfall formed east of the Georgia coast on the morning of January 27 and moved slowly northeast to a position east of Cape Hatteras on the morning of January 28. A large, nearly stationary high pressure system centered over the Saint Lawrence Valley provided a steady flow of cold air over the region to ensure the precipitation remained all snow. Every flake of snow accumulated on Washington, which would ultimately prove disastrous for those who attended the show at the Knickerbocker Theater on the evening of January 28.

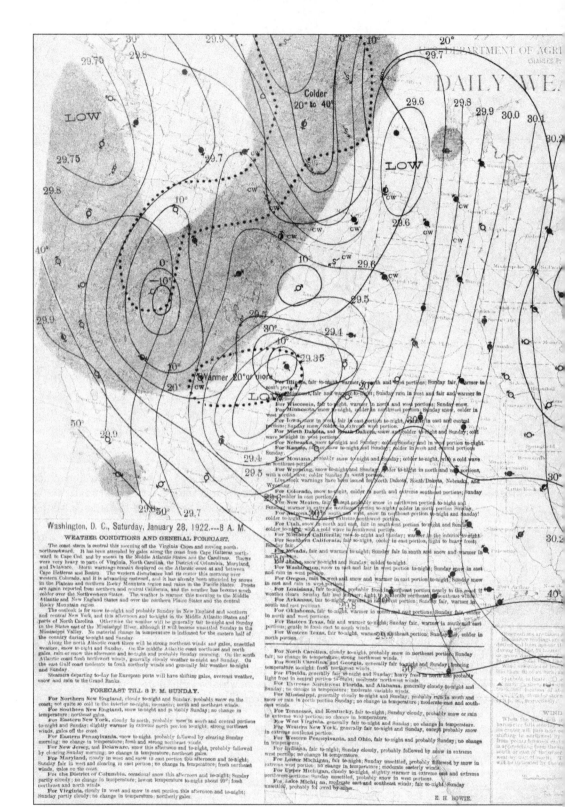

Washington, D. C., Saturday, January 28, 1922.—8 A. M.

## WEATHER CONDITIONS AND GENERAL FORECAST.

The coast storm is central this morning off the Virginia Capes and moving north-northeastward. It has been attended by gales along the coast from Cape Hatteras northward to Cape Cod, and by snows in the Middle Atlantic States and the Carolinas. Snows were very heavy in parts of Virginia, North Carolina, the District of Columbia, Maryland, and Delaware. Storm warnings remain displayed on the Atlantic coast at and between Cape Hatteras and Boston. The western disturbance had its center this morning over western Colorado, and it is advancing eastward, and it has already been attended by snows in the Plateau and northern Rocky Mountain region and rains in the Pacific States. Frosts are again reported from northern and central California, and the weather has become much colder over the Northwestern States. The weather is warmer this morning in the Middle Atlantic and New England States and over the northern Plains States and the central Rocky Mountain region.

The outlook is for snow to-night and probably Sunday in New England and southern and central New York, and this afternoon and to-night in the Middle Atlantic States and parts of North Carolina. Otherwise the weather will be generally fair to-night and Sunday in the States east of the Mississippi River, although it will become unsettled Sunday in the Mississippi Valley. No material change in temperature is indicated for the eastern half of the country during to-night and Sunday.

Along the north Atlantic coast there will be strong northeast winds and gales, unsettled weather, snow to-night and Sunday. On the middle Atlantic coast northeast and north gales, rain or snow this afternoon and to-night and probably Sunday morning. On the north Atlantic coast fresh northwest winds, generally cloudy weather to-night and Sunday. On the east Gulf coast moderate to fresh northerly winds and generally fair weather to-night and Sunday.

Steamers departing to-day for European ports will have shifting gales, overcast weather, snow and rain to the Grand Banks.

## FORECAST TILL 8 P. M. SUNDAY.

For Northern New England, cloudy to-night and Sunday, probably snow on the coast; not quite so cold in the interior to-night; increasing north and northeast winds.

For Southern New England, snow to-night and probably Sunday; no change in temperature; northeast gales.

For Eastern New York, cloudy in north, probably snow in south and central portions to-night and Sunday; slightly warmer in extreme north portion to-night, strong northeast winds, gales off the coast.

For Eastern Pennsylvania, snow to-night, probably followed by clearing Sunday morning; no change in temperature; fresh and strong northeast winds.

For New Jersey, and Delaware, snow this afternoon and to-night, probably followed by clearing Sunday morning; no change in temperature; northeast gales.

For Maryland, cloudy in west and snow in east portion this afternoon and to-night; Sunday fair in west and clearing in east portion; no change in temperature; fresh northeast winds, gales on the coast.

For the District of Columbia, occasional snow this afternoon and to-night; Sunday partly cloudy; no change in temperature; lowest temperature to-night about 20°; fresh northeast and north winds.

For Virginia, cloudy in west and snow in east portion this afternoon and to-night; Sunday partly cloudy; no change in temperature; northerly gales.

For Illinois, fair to-night, warmer in north and west portions; Sunday fair, warmer in south portion.

For Missouri, fair and warmer to-night; Sunday rain in west and fair and warmer in east.

For Wisconsin, fair to-night, warmer in north and west portions; Sunday snow.

For Minnesota, snow to-night, colder in northwest portion; Sunday snow, colder in west portion.

For Iowa, snow in west, fair in east portion to-night, warmer in east and central portions; Sunday snow, colder in extreme west portion.

For North Dakota, and South Dakota, snow and colder to-night and Sunday; cold wave to-night in west portion.

For Nebraska, snow to-night and Sunday; colder Sunday and in west portion to-night.

For Kansas, fair or snow to-night and Sunday; colder in west and central portions Sunday.

For Montana, probably snow to-night and Sunday; colder to-night, with a cold wave in southeast portion.

For Wyoming, snow to-night and Sunday; colder to-night in north and west portions, with a cold wave; colder Sunday in south portion.

Cold-wave warnings have been issued for North Dakota, South Dakota, Nebraska, and Wyoming.

For Colorado, snow to-night, colder in north and extreme southeast portions; Sunday colder in east portion.

For New Mexico, fair, except probably snow in northwest portion to-night and Sunday; warmer in extreme southeast portion to-night; colder in north portion Sunday.

For Arizona, fair in south and west, snow in northeast portion to-night and Sunday; colder to-night, with a cold wave in extreme northwest portion.

For Utah, snow in north and east, fair in southwest portion to-night and Sunday; colder to-night, with a cold wave in southwest portion.

For Northern California, rain to-night and Sunday; warmer in the interior to-night.

For Southern California, fair to-night, cooler in east portion, light to heavy frosts Sunday fair.

For Nevada, fair and warmer to-night; Sunday fair in south and snow and warmer in north portion.

For Idaho, snow to-night and Sunday; colder to-night.

For Washington, rain in east and fair in west portion to-night; Sunday snow in east and rain in west portion.

For Oregon, rain in west and snow and warmer in east portion to-night; Sunday snow in east and rain in west portion.

For Louisiana, fair to-night, probably frost in northeast portion nearly to the coast if weather clears Sunday fair and warmer; light to moderate northeast to southeast winds.

For Arkansas, fair to-night, warmer in northwest portion; Sunday fair, warmer in south and east portions.

For Oklahoma, fair to-night, warmer in south and east portions; Sunday fair, colder in north and west portions.

For Eastern Texas, fair and warmer to-night; Sunday fair, warmer in south and east portions; gentle to fresh east to south winds.

For Western Texas, fair to-night, warmer in southeast portion; Sunday fair, colder in north portion.

For North Carolina, cloudy to-night, probably snow in northeast portion; Sunday fair; no change in temperature; strong northwest winds.

For South Carolina and Georgia, generally fair to-night and Sunday; freezing temperature to-night; fresh northwest winds.

For Florida, generally fair to-night and Sunday; heavy frost in north and probably light frost in central portion to-night; moderate northwest winds.

For Extreme Northwest Florida, and Alabama, generally cloudy to-night and Sunday; no change in temperature; moderate variable winds.

For Mississippi, generally cloudy to-night and Sunday, probably rain in south and snow or rain in north portion Sunday; no change in temperature; moderate east and south-east winds.

For Tennessee, and Kentucky, fair to-night; Sunday cloudy, probably snow or rain in extreme west portion; no change in temperature.

For West Virginia, generally fair to-night and Sunday; no change in temperature.

For Western New York, generally fair to-night and Sunday, except probably snow in extreme northeast portion.

For Western Pennsylvania, and Ohio, fair to-night and probably Sunday; no change in temperature.

For Indiana, fair to-night; Sunday cloudy, probably followed by snow in extreme west portion; no change in temperature.

For Lower Michigan, fair to-night; Sunday unsettled, probably followed by snow in extreme west portion; no change in temperature; moderate easterly winds.

For Upper Michigan, cloudy to-night, slightly warmer in extreme east and extreme northwest portions; Sunday unsettled, probably snow in west portions.

For Lake Michigan, moderate east and southeast winds, fair to-night; Sunday unsettled, probably followed by snow.

E. H. BOWIE.

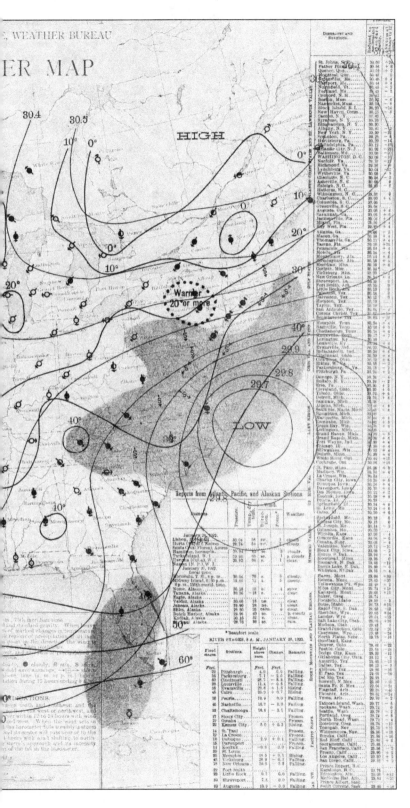

The surface weather map for January 28, 1922, shows the Knickerbocker Snowstorm east of Cape Hatteras, North Carolina. The storm did not move up the coast like a traditional nor'easter. Rather, once the storm reached the latitude of Cape Hatteras, North Carolina, it slid east-northeast out to sea. The storm dumped 28 inches of snow on Washington, which set the single storm snowfall record. The shaded area on the map represents precipitation. The text on the left describes the current weather conditions and outlines the weather forecast for regions of the United States. The forecast text also appears on pages 16 and 17 of this book. (NOAA Library.)

Pictured is a firefighter boat on the Potomac River the day before the Knickerbocker Snowstorm, January 26, 1922. Five days of cold weather preceded the storm and produced significant ice on the Potomac River. On the day of this photograph, the high temperature was 30 degrees, and the low temperature was 11 degrees. On the following day, light snow began to fall on Washington, ushering in the record-breaking snowstorm that would later collapse the roof of the Knickerbocker Theater and would give the snowstorm its namesake. (Library of Congress.)

These residents of Washington found excellent ice-skating conditions on Rock Creek the day before the Knickerbocker Snowstorm. Rock Creek was a favorite ice-skating destination during extended periods of cold weather. (Library of Congress.)

There was ice-skating on the Reflecting Pool and overcast skies from the approaching Knickerbocker Snowstorm. This photograph was taken on January 27, 1922, just before the first flakes of snow fell. Snow began in Washington later that afternoon, at about 4:00 p.m. The high temperature that day was 25 degrees, and the low was 18 degrees. (Library of Congress.)

A girl takes a sled out into the Knickerbocker Snowstorm on January 28, 1922. This sled appears to be a Coaster King from the Auto-Wheel Coaster Company. This is a common sled design of the period with its wooden steering handle also serving as the sled's bumper. The sled makes for a nice photograph, but runner sleds do not do well in fresh, deep powder. By mid-morning on January 28, the snow had already accumulated 20 inches in Washington, and the sledding opportunities for this young girl would have been quite limited. Another photograph shows her mother sitting on the sled (see page 26). (Library of Congress.)

A US Weather Bureau kiosk is buried by snow in Washington on January 28, 1922. This weather kiosk was located on Pennsylvania Avenue near E Street and was used to measure temperature, humidity, and rainfall. The Weather Bureau eventually became the National Weather Service by a presidential decree issued by Richard M. Nixon in 1970. (Library of Congress.)

Heavy snow falls on Washington near Pennsylvania Avenue. The storm responsible for the record snowfall formed east of the Georgia coast on the morning of January 27 and moved slowly north to a position east of Cape Hatteras on the morning of January 28. (Library of Congress.)

## Washington, D. C., Friday, January 27, 1922.---8 A. M.

### WEATHER CONDITIONS AND GENERAL FORECAST.

Pressure remains high over the Northeastern States, and it has fallen off the south Atlantic coast and in all-western districts. The storm off the south Atlantic coast has been attended by general snows and rains in the South Atlantic and east Gulf States, Tennessee, eastern Arkansas, and southern Missouri, and a disturbance over the far Northwest is causing rains on the north California coast, and snows and rains in Washington and Oregon and northern Idaho. The temperature has risen slightly in nearly all districts east of the Mississippi River and in the Northwest, but temperatures remain below the normal throughout the Eastern and Southern States. Freezing temperatures prevail this morning as far south as extreme northern Florida, and the lowest temperature reported was 22° below zero at Northfield, Vt.

The outlook is for snow to-night and Saturday in southern New England, southern New York, the Middle Atlantic States, and West Virginia, and this afternoon and to-night in North Carolina, extreme northern South Carolina, and the extreme east portions of Tennessee and Kentucky. In other regions east of the Mississippi River the weather will be fair to-night and Saturday. The temperature will rise somewhat to-night in the interior of the Middle Atlantic States, the interior of New York, and the interior of New England. Temperature changes elsewhere east of the Mississippi River will be unimportant.

Storm warnings remain displayed on the Atlantic coast at and between the Virginia Capes and Cape Hatteras.

The winds along the north Atlantic coast will be increasing north and northeast, unsettled weather, snow over south portion to-night and Saturday. On the middle Atlantic coast increasing northeast winds, probably becoming gales; snow to-night and Saturday. On the south Atlantic coast fresh and strong shifting winds, becoming northwest and west; rain to-night, clearing Saturday. On the east Gulf coast moderate northerly winds and generally cloudy weather to-night and Saturday.

Steamers departing to-day for European ports will have strong east to north winds and gales, unsettled weather and snow to the Grand Banks.

### FORECAST TILL 8 P. M. SATURDAY.

For Northern New England, unsettled to-night and Saturday, rising temperature in Vermont and New Hampshire; fresh north to east winds.

For Southern New England, increasing cloudiness, snow late to-night or Saturday; rising temperature on the mainland; increasing northeast winds.

For Eastern New York, cloudy, snow in south portion to-night and Saturday; slowly rising temperature in the interior; increasing northeast and east winds.

For Eastern Pennsylvania, snow to-night and Saturday; not quite so cold to-night; increasing northeast winds.

For New Jersey, snow to-night and Saturday; slowly rising temperature; increasing northeast winds.

For Delaware, and Maryland, snow to-night and Saturday; no change in temperature; increasing northeast winds.

For the District of Columbia, snow to-night and probably Saturday; no change in temperature; lowest temperature to-night about 20°; increasing northeast winds.

For Virginia, snow or rain on the coast and snow in the interior this afternoon and to-night; warmer in southwest portion to-night; Saturday clearing; strong northeast winds and probably gales.

For North Carolina, rain on the coast and snow in the interior this afternoon and to-night; colder on the coast to-night; Saturday fair, with rising temperature in the interior; fresh and strong east to north winds.

The Weather Bureau issued the weather conditions and general forecast on Friday, January 27, 1922, at 8:00 a.m. The forecast for Washington was "snow to-night and probably Saturday; no change in temperature; increasing northeast winds." It was noted that steamers departing for European ports would encounter strong east-to-north gales and unsettled weather with snow. (NOAA Library.)

16

# Washington, D. C., Saturday, January 28, 1922.---8 A. M.

## WEATHER CONDITIONS AND GENERAL FORECAST.

The coast storm is central this morning off the Virginia Capes and moving north-northeastward. It has been attended by gales along the coast from Cape Hatteras northward to Cape Cod, and by snows in the Middle Atlantic States and the Carolinas. Snows were very heavy in parts of Virginia, North Carolina, the District of Columbia, Maryland, and Delaware. Storm warnings remain displayed on the Atlantic coast at and between Cape Hatteras and Boston. The western disturbance had its center this morning over western Colorado, and it is advancing eastward, and it has already been attended by snows in the Plateau and northern Rocky Mountain region and rains in the Pacific States. Frosts are again reported from northern and central California, and the weather has become much colder over the Northwestern States. The weather is warmer this morning in the Middle Atlantic and New England States and over the northern Plains States and the central Rocky Mountain region.

The outlook is for snow to-night and probably Sunday in New England and southern and central New York, and this afternoon and to-night in the Middle Atlantic States and parts of North Carolina. Otherwise the weather will be generally fair to-night and Sunday in the States east of the Mississippi River, although it will become unsettled Sunday in the Mississippi Valley. No material change in temperature is indicated for the eastern half of the country during to-night and Sunday.

Along the north Atlantic coast there will be strong northeast winds and gales, unsettled weather, snow to-night and Sunday. On the middle Atlantic coast northeast and north gales, rain or snow this afternoon and to-night and probably Sunday morning. On the south Atlantic coast fresh northwest winds, generally cloudy weather to-night and Sunday. On the east Gulf coast moderate to fresh northerly winds and generally fair weather to-night and Sunday.

Steamers departing to-day for European ports will have shifting gales, overcast weather, snow and rain to the Grand Banks.

## FORECAST TILL 8 P. M. SUNDAY.

**For Northern New England,** cloudy to-night and Sunday, probably snow on the coast; not quite so cold in the interior to-night; increasing north and northeast winds.

**For Southern New England,** snow to-night and probably Sunday; no change in temperature; northeast gales.

**For Eastern New York,** cloudy in north, probably snow in south and central portions to-night and Sunday; slightly warmer in extreme north portion to-night; strong northeast winds, gales off the coast.

**For Eastern Pennsylvania,** snow to-night, probably followed by clearing Sunday morning; no change in temperature; fresh and strong northeast winds.

**For New Jersey, and Delaware,** snow this afternoon and to-night, probably followed by clearing Sunday morning; no change in temperature; northeast gales.

**For Maryland,** cloudy in west and snow in east portion this afternoon and to-night; Sunday fair in west and clearing in east portion; no change in temperature; fresh northeast winds, gales on the coast.

**For the District of Columbia,** occasional snow this afternoon and to-night; Sunday partly cloudy; no change in temperature; lowest temperature to-night about 20°; fresh northeast and north winds.

**For Virginia,** cloudy in west and snow in east portion this afternoon and to-night; Sunday partly cloudy; no change in temperature; northerly gales.

The Weather Bureau issued the weather conditions and general forecast on Saturday, January 28, 1922, at 8:00 a.m. The forecast for Washington was "occasional snow this afternoon and to-night; Sunday partly cloudy; no change in temperature." It was noted that the storm was moving away from the Virginia Capes and heading north-northeastward. (NOAA Library.)

17

Washington streetcars struggled to run during the heavy snow that fell on January 28, 1922. In the photograph, a milk and bread truck is parked in the snow. The official snow recorded in Washington was 28 inches, measured at Twenty-fourth and M Streets NW, a single storm snowfall record that still holds today. (Library of Congress.)

A car is hopelessly stuck and abandoned in the snow. Meanwhile, streetcars were struggling to keep running. The snow was surpassing 20 inches at the time of this photograph, and about eight inches of additional accumulation was yet to fall. The temperature rose to the freezing point by the end of the storm. (Library of Congress.)

Pictured is a streetcar sweeper in front of the Café Lorraine on 1409 H Street NW. The sweepers were used to keep tracks clear, but they could not keep up with the fast accumulating snow. As a result, many of the streetcars got stuck in the snow. In addition, the trains between Washington and Alexandria stopped running because of deep snow and drifts on the tracks. (Library of Congress.)

Cars are buried in snow during the Knickerbocker Snowstorm. Temperatures hovered in the 20s for the majority of the storm but slowly rose to 31 degrees as the snow ended. The temperature during the height of the storm was 25 degrees. (Library of Congress.)

A truck and streetcar meet in a cleared section of road. Roads became impassible with heavy snow accumulation on January 28, 1922. The Washington Terminal officials put out a hurry call for shovelers to clear the railroad yards. The city's street-cleaning department announced they were in need of an additional 150 laborers to shovel snow from the streets. Meanwhile, the refuse

department directed all employees to work on shoveling and clearing the snow from streets before clearing trash. Sweeper cars helped to clear the tracks, and shovelers managed to keep a few roads open during the storm. Because of the bad road conditions, many people chose to walk to their destinations, including the Knickerbocker Theater. (Library of Congress.)

A streetcar sweeper pushes through the thick snow on a Washington street during the morning of January 28, 1922. (Library of Congress.)

An empty streetcar is pictured in heavy snow near New York Avenue and Fourteenth Street. A large, high-pressure system, centered over the Saint Lawrence Valley, provided a steady flow of cold air over the region to ensure the precipitation remained all snow. (Library of Congress.)

Pictured is a street scene in Washington on January 28, 1922. (Library of Congress.)

People boarded a streetcar that was kept running on January 28, 1922. Sweeper cars ran to clear the tracks while crews worked to keep switches working. (Library of Congress.)

A car is buried deep in the snow. A photograph would later be taken of the owner starting the long task of digging out the car (see page 31). (Library of Congress.)

Leaving a car's top down on January 28, 1922, undoubtedly created a large cleanup job for this car's owner. The inside of the car collected 28 inches of heavy, wet snow. The weather forecasts of 1922 did not mention snow accumulations, most likely surprising this car's owner. (Library of Congress.)

A woman is carried across a snow-covered street on January 28, 1922. This photograph was included on a page of the Weather Bureau's photograph book *The Storm*, which commemorates the Knickerbocker Snowstorm. The original caption read, "Fording the Deep Snow." (NOAA Library.)

A young girl and her mom try to sled on January 28, 1922. (Library of Congress.)

Two young ladies are bundled up to keep warm in the blowing snow as the temperature stayed below freezing on January 28, 1922. (Library of Congress.)

The same young ladies pose on a snowbank on January 28, 1922. Most of the roads in Washington were made impassable by the heavy snowfall. (Library of Congress.)

This is another photograph of the two young ladies in the snow. (Library of Congress.)

This policeman is standing on a snow pile directing traffic on January 28, 1922. This must have been staged, since not much traffic was moving on the snow-choked streets at the time. In a matter of hours, the police would be called to the Knickerbocker Theater for a rescue effort. (Library of Congress.)

Across the Potomac River in Alexandria, Virginia, the deep snow prevented firemen from responding to a fire at St. Paul's Church. The fire engine got stuck in the snow one block from the church, and the firemen could not find the fireplugs under the deep snow. The blaze was blamed on a snow-clogged chimney. (Alexandria Library Special Collections.)

The White House is pictured during the Knickerbocker Snowstorm. Pres. Warren G. Harding was at the White House during the storm. Harding was the 29th president of the United States (1921–1923). The vice president was Calvin Coolidge. (Library of Congress.)

A car is parked outside the front entrance of the White House during the Knickerbocker Snowstorm. Travel in the city was extremely difficult during the storm, with few roads and rails open for travel. (Library of Congress.)

A man is only half visible in deep snow outside of the Smithsonian Institute as the snowfall has ended. The storm itself was remarkable for its persevering intensity, generating snowfall rates of greater than one inch per hour over the 24-hour period from Friday afternoon, January 27 through Saturday afternoon, January 28. A total of 25 inches of snow fell in that span, establishing a 24-hour snowfall record. The overall storm total was 28 inches, which still holds the single storm record in Washington. Because the official snow measuring location for Washington was moved from Twenty-fourth and M Streets NW to near sea level at Washington Reagan National Airport, it will be especially difficult for another snowstorm to break the record. (Library of Congress.)

The Nordlinger brothers, Wolf and Bernard, owned stores on M Street in Georgetown. Wolf owned a clothing store, and Bernard owned a shoe store. In this photograph, Wolf, his son, and his nephews clear snow from in front of their clothing store after the Knickerbocker Snowstorm. (Robin Nordlinger Leiman.)

Pictured is a woman beginning to dig out a car on January 28, 1922. The snow was about two feet deep at the time of this photograph. Shoveling snow is still the same chore as it was in 1922. (NOAA Library.)

This photograph of the Department of Treasury building appeared on the cover of a book about the Knickerbocker Snowstorm. *The Storm* was a small book of about 20 photographs and brief captions. This copy of the book was put into the Weather Bureau's library and was stamped February 11, 1922. (NOAA Library.)

Pictured is New York Avenue and Fourteenth Street during the Knickerbocker Snowstorm on January 28, 1922. This photograph was included in *The Storm*. The original caption reads, "New York Avenue and Fourteenth Street." (NOAA Library.)

Pictured is Pennsylvania Avenue during the Knickerbocker Snowstorm on January 28, 1922. The original caption reads, "Pennsylvania Avenue near State, War, and Navy Building." (NOAA Library.)

Pictured is pedestrian activity on F Street during the Knickerbocker Snowstorm on January 28, 1922. The original caption reads, "F Street, Washington's Busiest Thoroughfare." (NOAA Library.)

Pictured is Lafayette Square during the Knickerbocker Snowstorm on January 28, 1922. The original caption reads, "Scene in Lafayette Square During the Storm." (NOAA Library.)

This photograph shows people walking to work or running errands during the storm on January 28, 1922. The original caption reads, "The Only Method of Getting to Work Saturday Morning." (NOAA Library.)

This photograph shows people slipping or falling during the Knickerbocker Snowstorm on January 28, 1922. The original caption as it appears in *The Storm* reads, "Slippery Walks Were Responsible for Many Falls." (NOAA Library.)

A few ladies are pictured having fun in the snow on January 28, 1922. This photograph was taken before the theater disaster. The original caption as it appears in *The Storm* reads, "The Snow Brought Joy to Some." (NOAA Library.)

This is a photograph of King Street in Alexandria, Virginia, soon after the snowstorm ended on January 29, 1922. It was noted that "the trolley line is having a hard time keeping their tracks clear." Over 150 men were put to work digging out Alexandria's rail lines, streets, and fireplugs. (Alexandria Library Special Collections.)

This is a photograph of Fifteenth Street and Pennsylvania Avenue on January 28, 1922. The original caption reads, "Fifteenth Street and Pennsylvania Avenue." (NOAA Library.)

Pictured are men trying to keep the streetcar switches in operation. The original caption reads, "Thawing Switches—Every Effort Was Made to Keep Cars Running." (NOAA Library.)

Only a few streets and rail lines were kept open during the snowstorm. By mid-afternoon on January 28, the snow reached a depth of 25 inches and shut down most travel throughout the Washington area. This photograph shows a car still able to navigate Washington's streets on January 28, 1922. (Library of Congress.)

This photograph shows the exterior of the Knickerbocker Theater on the night of the disaster, which occurred on January 28, 1922. By midnight, thousands of Washingtonians had heard of the theater's roof collapse, and all roads that led to the Knickerbocker Theater were filled with curious people who wanted to see the rescue effort or people who believed that they might have had a friend or family member in the theater. The homes that were near the theater had a constant flow of people asking to use the telephone to call home to check on loved ones, to make sure that they had not gone to the theater that night. (NOAA Library.)

# Two

# DISASTER AT THE THEATER

On the evening of Saturday January 28, 1922, several hundred people fought their way through a massive snowstorm to watch films at the Knickerbocker Theater, Washington's largest and most modern moving picture theater of the time.

Saturday night was comedy night at the Knickerbocker Theater, and *Get-Rich-Quick Wallingford* was the featured film that evening. The first movie that night, *School Days*, was a 1921 silent picture starring freckle-faced boy actor Wesley Barry, and it had drawn many Washington-area children to the theater to watch the film. Shortly before 9:00 p.m., the theater's orchestra finished playing for intermission, and the featured movie was just starting to roll.

As *Get-Rich-Quick Wallingford* began and the first laughs came from the audience, a loud hissing noise was heard from above. The ceiling, weighed down from the snow, had begun to split apart down the middle. Many people, including the children in the audience, noticed the splitting ceiling and falling plaster chunks and dove under their seats or ran for the door. Within seconds, the entire roof pulled free from the theater's brick walls and plunged down toward the crowd. As the roof fell, it collapsed the theater's cement balcony and also pulled down portions of the theater's brick walls. Chunks of concrete, bricks, and twisted steel beams crashed to the theater floor, burying the movie patrons.

A chaotic rescue effort began with survivors and volunteers on the street. It became better organized when the police, marines, and firemen arrived on the scene. Police lines were drawn and heavy equipment was summoned. A fleet of ambulances arrived from Walter Reed Army Medical Center to help evacuate the injured to hospitals.

By midnight, 200 police, soldiers, and firemen were working feverishly, digging through the wreckage. By 2:30 a.m., over 600 rescue workers were on the scene. Residents in the vicinity of the theater supplied hot food and coffee to the rescuers. The rescue effort continued into the afternoon of the following day.

The toll for the disaster was 98 dead and 133 injured. Every hospital in the area was filled with the injured. Many stores and houses served as short-term first aid stations. Hotels opened their doors to the injured as well as the rescue workers. The disaster ranks as one of the worst in Washington's history.

# The Washington Post.

NO. 16,664. DAILY AND SUNDAY · WASHINGTON: SUNDAY, JANUARY 29, 1922. · FIVE CENTS.

## HUNDREDS, DEAD OR INJURED, BURIED UNDER RUINS AS ROOF OF KNICKERBOCKER THEATER COLLAPSES; RESCUERS BATTLE STORM THAT PARALYZES CITY

### Bodies of 25 Victims Recovered; 55 Wounded Dragged From Debris; Frantic Search for 8 Missing

**Relatives Weep in Vain at Yawning Doors of Wrecked Building**

**DOCTORS INSTALL HOSPITAL IN NEARBY CANDY STORE**

*Grim Tragedy Descends on Light-Hearted Crowd Gathered to View Film Comedy. Wife Carried Out and Laid Dying at Husband's Feet—Ambulances Race Through Snow-Drifted Streets to Carry Away Injured—Second Assistant Postmaster General Shaughnessy and Wife and Daughter Among Those Hurt.*

### HORROR HAMPERS AID AS VOLUNTEERS DIG

### REMOVAL OF SNOW IS DUTY OF CITIZENS

**"Do It Today," Is Appeal of Federation's President**

### BLIZZARD COSTS 1 LIFE; CAPITAL GOES AFOOT; BUSINESS IS HALTED

**Washington Center of Driving Blizzard That Sweeps Virginia, Maryland and Delaware—Snowfall Exceeds All Records Except Big Storm of 1899—Capital Paralyzed Under Deep Blanket of White.**

---

### DEAD, MISSING AND INJURED

#### THE IDENTIFIED DEAD

#### UNIDENTIFIED

#### MISSING

#### THE INJURED

---

Pictured is the front page of the *Washington Post* on Sunday, January 29, 1922. The newspapers covered the Knickerbocker Theater Disaster in great detail and focused on many different stories of mourning and rescue as well as tales of tragic death and dismemberment. The common man was made the focus of the articles over the politicians and prominent businessmen, who also suffered injury and death in the theater. The names of dead, injured, and missing were listed daily. One reporter on the scene wrote, "People in the theater went to see a comedy but ended up in a tragedy." The record-breaking snowstorm was also covered in the newspaper but as a secondary news item to the Knickerbocker Disaster. (Author's collection.)

Soldiers and police are pictured in front of the Knickerbocker Theater during the rescue effort. Police, soldiers, and firemen worked feverishly to dig through the wreckage. The roof, burdened by the weight of the heavy snow, collapsed on the moviegoers. As the roof fell, it collapsed the theater's cement balcony and also pulled down portions of the theater's brick walls. (Library of Congress.)

Bystanders and ambulances are pictured outside the Knickerbocker Theater on January 29, 1922. The toll for the disaster was 98 dead and 133 injured. Every hospital in the area was filled with the injured, and many stores and houses served as short-term first-aid stations. A temporary hospital was set up in a nearby candy store. (Library of Congress.)

This is a view from above of the police line showing spectators outside the Knickerbocker Theater during the rescue effort. Hundreds of Washington-area citizens gathered to watch the scene as police, firemen, and soldiers dug through the rubble of what had once been the roof and balcony of the Knickerbocker Theater. (Library of Congress.)

Pictured are a fire engine and ambulances outside of the Knickerbocker Theater on January 29, 1922. A fleet of ambulances with support staff and nurses arrived from Walter Reed Army Medical Center to help move the injured to area hospitals. The disaster ranks as one of the worst in Washington's history. (Library of Congress.)

Two nurses stand outside the Knickerbocker Theater next to ambulances from Walter Reed Army Medical Center. The *Washington Post* described how men on the rescue teams gave a "superhuman" effort to dig through the "stern steel and timber" of the wrecked theater "with sober earnestness." (The Historical Society of Washington, DC.)

Pictured are piles of rubble and debris outside of the Knickerbocker Theater. Chunks of concrete, bricks, and twisted steel beams crashed to the theater floor, burying the movie patrons. The newspapers described how grown men would break down and sob as they uncovered the horrors buried below the theater's collapsed roof and balcony. (Library of Congress.)

Wrecked interior of the Knickerbocker Theatre, Washington, the morning after the snow-laden roof collapsed, bringing death and injury to scores sitting in the audience beneath. The disaster occurred on the night of Jan. 28, 1922.

United States Marines and firemen of Washington digging in the debris for victims of the Knickerbocker Theatre collapse, many whom were buried beneath the ruins for the entire night.

In 1922, the *American Pictorial Magazine* featured two photographs from the Knickerbocker Theater's wrecked interior. The title of the page reads, "Nearly One Hundred Killed by Theatre Roof Collapse." The first caption reads, "Wrecked interior of the Knickerbocker Theatre, Washington, the morning after the snow-laden roof collapsed, bringing death and injury to scores sitting in the audience beneath. The disaster occurred the night of Jan. 28, 1922." The second caption reads, "United States Marines and firemen of Washington digging in the debris for victims of the Knickerbocker Theater collapse, many whom were buried beneath the ruins for the entire night." (Author's collection.)

Soldiers work to clear wreckage and remove the dead and injured from inside the Knickerbocker Theater. Several hours after the roof collapsed, over 200 police, soldiers, and firemen arrived at the scene. By early in the morning of January 29, over 600 rescue workers were on the scene. (The Historical Society of Washington, DC.)

Soldiers carry the dead and injured from the Knickerbocker Theater. The clubhouse of the nearby Town and Country Club served as a headquarters for the rescue effort, where workers were able to eat, drink, and rest. Several members of the country club were on the list of dead after the roof collapse. (Library of Congress.)

Soldiers carry the dead and injured from the Knickerbocker Theater. Initially, after the Knickerbocker Theater's roof collapsed, a chaotic rescue effort began with survivors and volunteers on the street helping uncover the victims in the rubble. The rescue effort became better organized when the police, marines, and firemen arrived on the scene. The rescue effort continued into the afternoon of January 30. (Both, Library of Congress.)

Soldiers carry victims of the Knickerbocker Theater Disaster in and out of a temporary morgue. The morgue was set up in the basement of the Christian Science Church, which was located near the theater. The *Washington Post* described many "pathetic scenes as men and women identified their sons, daughters, mothers, wives, and sweethearts among the dead." People "besieged" the morgue, trying to discover news of friends and family members who had been identified as missing in the disaster. (Both, Library of Congress.)

A fireman or rescue worker organizes what appears to be a long hose outside of the Knickerbocker Theater. The worker is inside the police lines and is visible and being watched by hundreds of spectators that were kept behind long police lines that circled the Knickerbocker Theater. (The Historical Society of Washington, DC.)

*The Knickerbocker Newsreel*

A silent newsreel was produced that shows the Knickerbocker Theater rescue effort. It shows rescue workers digging through the collapsed roof and spectators behind police lines. It also shows people rushing in and out of the theater and a fire engine driving by the theater. The newsreel can be watched on YouTube. (Barry Reichenbaugh.)

# *Three*

# KNICKERBOCKER STORIES

Dorsey Bush, an operator for the Chesapeake and Potomac Telephone Company, received a frantic call shortly after 9:00 p.m. "My name is Norris. The roof the Knickerbocker Theater has caved in. Send the nearest doctor." The operator immediately called the police department and hospitals, alerting them to the disaster. Six other operators were then assigned to call every doctor in the area. A total of 72 doctors were called to respond to the Knickerbocker Theater that evening. The operator was later given an award for her quick thinking.

Mary Forsyth was pinned under the wreckage of the Knickerbocker Theater's roof. Next to Mary was a young couple, "a man and his sweetheart," who were also pinned under the concrete. While moans of pain and anguish could be heard from all sides, the man began to sing. His girl joined in song. Both sang for many minutes until they lapsed into unconsciousness and passed away. Mary Forsyth survived and would tell the story of the singing couple. It was later learned that a couple on their honeymoon perished that night in the theater. It may have been the same couple.

A Mr. Theunissen was sitting next to his daughter when he heard a great crash. A falling block of concrete then knocked him unconscious. When he awakened, he could hear his daughter calling, "Daddy, Daddy, Daddy." He then heard, "Please save my Daddy." He rigorously searched the wreckage from where he heard her voice. Four volunteers joined him in the search. Later, Mr. Theunissen gave up and went home "broken-hearted." At home, he found his daughter waiting. She had been carried home much earlier by a rescue worker. She was unharmed.

Agnes Mellon was on a date at the Knickerbocker Theater. Suddenly, the theater's roof collapsed. As the roof crashed to the floor, a terrible gust of wind blew outward as the air inside the theater was violently evacuated. Agnes's date was blown into the lobby and saved from the crushing debris. Agnes did not survive. Agnes was later identified in the morgue by her khaki knickerbockers, a sad irony.

As the rescuers dug through the rubble, they found a large air pocket that had been created by the roof's steel beams that had buckled upward. In the middle of the air pocket was a man sitting upright in his theater chair, untouched and uninjured by the collapsed roof. He was dead, however, a victim of an apparent heart attack.

The Knickerbocker Theater's orchestra pit is seen before and after the collapse of the roof. Six of the 11 musicians in the orchestra were killed. A few of the orchestra members were partially protected by lying down next to the stage. (Library of Congress.)

Police, soldiers, and firemen examine the rubble and wreckage inside the Knickerbocker Theater during the rescue effort. Chunks of concrete, bricks, and twisted steel beams crashed to the theater floor, burying the movie patrons. Some people were buried for almost a day. (Library of Congress.)

The rescue team surveys the damage inside the Knickerbocker Theater. Soldiers from nearby bases were called to help. Many soldiers brought gas masks because rumors spread that the gas lines going into the theater had ruptured. The gas masks were discarded when it was learned the odor of gas was from the firemen's acetylene torches. (Library of Congress.)

This is a close up of rescue workers inside the Knickerbocker Theater after the roof collapse. The construction men who responded to the disaster said they could not give an estimate to the weight that had fallen on the several hundred heads in the audience. Later, the opinion was offered that the roof could have weighed between 2 and 10 tons. (Library of Congress.)

This is a view inside the Knickerbocker Theater during the rescue effort. It was noted that the roof came down in a flat surface, no corner remained suspended. The entire length and width of the roof buckled and fell at once together and crashed to the floor of the theater. It was the worst possible scenario for the people inside. (Library of Congress.)

Pictured is the police line outside of the Knickerbocker Theater. The *Washington Post* wrote, "The thousands of persons who assembled on the streets near the outside of the theater could have no idea of what happened inside. There was no way of telling that a tragedy had occurred, save that great crowds had gathered and police and firemen were working like fury." (Library of Congress.)

This is a wide view inside the Knickerbocker Theater during the rescue effort. When the roof crashed to the ground, a strong gust of wind blew outward as the air inside the theater was violently evacuated. Some people in the back of the theater were blown clear of the falling roof. One lady was blown through a window and was saved from the crushing rubble. (Library of Congress.)

After the rescue effort, a couple of investigators stand on what was the Knickerbocker's stage. One survivor, a Mrs. Knessi, insisted to her family that they not sit by the stage but instead sit at the back of the theater. She credited her lifelong aversion to sitting in the front of the theater with saving her life. Her husband and son, however, were killed in the roof collapse. (Library of Congress.)

Pictured are soldiers searching through the rubble for survivors and uncovering the dead. When one rescue worker became tired and wanted to quit, another worker was overheard saying, "Go in there and look at that boy trapped under the roof. Go and see the determination on his face. Then, quit if you want to, but you can't!" The tired rescue worker went back to work. (Library of Congress.)

This is a close-up view of the twisted steel beams and roof materials that plunged to the ground on top of hundreds of moviegoers. At times, a small boy was sent into the holes and openings of the tangled wreckage to deliver water and pain pills to the victims buried underneath. The large sections of concrete were difficult to move, and some victims stayed buried for many hours. (Library of Congress.)

Rescue workers are pictured among building materials that had once been the theater's roof and balcony. The people in the first few rows of the balcony were catapulted out of their seats and landed on the heads of moviegoers in the front rows of the theater. An instant later, the roof crashed down on everyone. (Library of Congress.)

Rescuers were all classes of people, including workmen, clerks, priests, and police officers. One man explained that he had just come from a poker party at a nearby apartment when he heard of the disaster and joined in the rescue effort. (Library of Congress.)

The Knickerbocker Theater's curtains will never close again. One reporter from the *Washington Post* wrote, "There was applause and laughter following a particularly clever comedy situation. There was a crash that struck terror into the hearts a-thrill with merriment. There was a gust of wind, a rushing of air that blew open the closed doors of the theater—and then, after one concerted groan, there was silence—and Crandall's Knickerbocker theatre, previously the temple of mirth, had been transformed into a tomb." Theater patrons sitting closest to the stage suffered the full brunt of the falling roof. Six members of the orchestra perished in the disaster. (Library of Congress.)

Police officers take a break for tea or coffee during the clean-up effort of the Knickerbocker Theater. Judging by the officer's expressions and casual appearance, the last body must have been removed long before this photograph was taken. It was a much different and more frantic scene in the hours that followed the theater's roof collapse. During the early morning of January 29, there were over 600 rescue workers were on the scene, composed of police, soldiers, firemen, and civilian volunteers. Residents in the vicinity of the theater supplied hot food and coffee to the rescuers. The rescue effort continued into the late afternoon, but clean up of the Knickerbocker Theater lasted for many weeks. (Library of Congress.)

Hundreds of spectators surround the Knickerbocker Theater during the rescue effort. Immediately after the roof collapsed, the cars along the surrounding streets had their jacks and tire irons stripped away to be used as tools for helping dig out the survivors. Once police lines were formed and order was restored, large saws were brought in to cut through the roof's heavy wire screen that held the ceiling's plaster. After the roof was removed, the workers used chisels and hydraulic jacks to break apart and move the cement structure of the balcony. (Library of Congress.)

David H. Lyman Jr., a 17-year-old Western High School student, went to the Knickerbocker Theater with a friend to watch silent films on the evening of January 28, 1922. David and his friend did not survive the crash of the roof. David's high school basketball team had an outing planned that night at the Knickerbocker Theater, but most of the boys could not make it due to the storm. (Frank Lyman.)

Agnes Mellon went on a date to the Knickerbocker Theater on the evening of January 28, 1922. When the roof crashed down, Agnes's boyfriend was blown into the lobby and landed unharmed. Agnes remained in the theater and was crushed. Agnes was later identified in the morgue by her khaki knickerbockers. Agnes was only 19 years old. (John Madert.)

The Knickerbocker Theater's orchestra conductor, Ernesto Natiello, was conducting when the roof came down. Ernesto and six members of the orchestra were killed. Ernesto's brother Oreste, a violin player in the orchestra, lost an arm in the disaster. (Nick Barkas.)

Col. George S. Patton led 100 men from Fort Myer to help with the rescue effort in the Knickerbocker Theater. Four teams of mules were needed to pull the Army trucks through the deep snow to reach the theater. Patton was unmoved by the horror he witnessed inside the theater. He would later tell his kids in great detail about the victims he found buried under the theater's rubble, much to the dismay of his wife, Beatrice. (Library of Congress.)

At right is the seating area and stage of the Knickerbocker Theater before the disaster. This photograph shows the ceiling that crashed down with the roof on the hundreds of people watching the silent films. (Library of Congress.)

Below is the exterior of the Knickerbocker Theater before the disaster. A year after the disaster, the Ambassador Theater would be built on the site and opened in September 1923. (Library of Congress.)

**Identified Dead in  Knickerbocker Theater Disaster**
**List from January 29, 1922**

Atkinson, Mary Ethel
Baker, Albert
Barchfeld, A. J.
Barchfeld, Miss Helena
Beal, Joseph W.
Bell, Archie
Bikle, William G.
Bikle, Miss M. C.
Bikle, Miss Frances
Bourne, Thomas R.
Bowden, Mrs. Daisy Garvey
Brainerd, C. C.
Brainerd, Mrs. C. C.
Brosseau, "Doc"
Buehler, Albert
Covell, Mrs. B. H.
Crawford, W. N.
Crocker, W. M.
Dauber, Vinson W.
Dorsey, Thomas M.
Dorsch, Miss Helen
Duke, Kirkland
Dutch, Miss Margaret
Eldridge, A. G.
Edridge, Guy S.
Ernst, F. H.
Farr, M. C.
Farraud, Mrs. Virginia
Feige, Christian
Fleming, John P.
Fleming, Miss Mary Lee
Fleming, Thomas.
Foster, Miss Esther
Freeman, G. S.
Gearhart, Mrs. Clyde M.
Hall, F. H.
Hillyer, Douglas
Hughes, William G.
Jackson, Daniel K.
Jeffries, Miss Elizabeth
Jeffries, John M.
Kanston, Oscar G.
Kanston, Mrs. Oscar G.
Kanston, Helen
Kanston, Anlyn
Kneesi, Howard W.
Kneesi, Howard Jr.
Laflin, Cutler
Lambert, Miss Nannie Lee
Lamby, Paulus
Lehler, L. L.
Lehmer, Leroy

Lehmer, Mrs. Leroy
Lyman, David H.
Maine, Russell.
Maine, Mrs. Russell
Matellio, Ernest E.
Martindale, Mrs. Norman E
Mckimlie, Jack
Mckimlie, Wyatt
Mckinney, Julian
Mellon, Miss Agnes
Mirsky, Mrs. Jean
Montgomery, Scott
Murphy, Miss Veronica
Murray, James W.
Ogden, Mrs. Vivian
O'donnell, D. F.
O'donnell, Mrs. D. F.
Parson, Mrs. Carrie
Pitcher, Miss Lois
Price, Hazel
Russell, Mrs. Marie
Sammon, W. B.
Scoofield, W. L.
Shea, Dr. James F.
Sigourney, Mrs. Cora C.
Smith, Miss Marie H.
Sproul, Laverne
Stephenson, C. E.
Strayer, L. W.
Sturgin, Victor M.
Taylor, Mrs. Gertrude
Tracey, William
Thompson, Christine
Thoms, Miss Gladys
Tucker, Col. Charles Cowles
Tucker, Mrs. Helen Miller
Urdong, Jacob
Urdong, Mrs. Jacob
Vallyntine, Louis F.
Vallyntine, Mrs. Louis F.
Vance, H. Conroy
Vance, Mrs. H. Conroy
Walford, Mildred
Walker, John L.
Walker, Mrs. Agnes
Walters, William
Walsh, D. N.
Walsh, Miss M. E.
Warner, Capt. William E. R.
Warner, Mrs. William E. R.
Wesson, Mrs. Charles M.
White, Ivan J.

A list of the identified dead from the Knickerbocker Theater Disaster was composed on January 29, 1922, and was published a day later. The list includes a former congressman from Pennsylvania and his daughter, six members of the orchestra, correspondents from New York and Pittsburgh, and many children. This list of 104 names was later reduced to 98, as a few of the identified dead were still living. One man on the list of dead remarked, "Friends who call my wife to express their sorrow at my death are disconcerted when I answer the telephone."

# Four

# THE AFTERMATH

Immediately following the Knickerbocker Theater Disaster, all Washington-area theaters were closed to prevent a similar incident. No other theater roofs caved in, however.

The collapse of the Knickerbocker Theater's roof brought nationwide attention to building codes and practices of large structures. An investigation followed, conducted by Congress, the city, and the courts. The investigations concluded that faulty design and construction of the Knickerbocker Theater was responsible for the roof collapse. The courts, however, were unable to determine who was liable.

After the disaster, the family of 17-year-old victim David Lyman sued the Knickerbocker Theater Company. The family lost the lawsuit, and the decision was later upheld by the Court of Appeals in *Lyman v. Knickerbocker Theatre Company* (1925). In the end, all of the Knickerbocker families lost their lawsuits.

In the days that followed the snowstorm, the city focused on digging out the streets and rail lines. The Washington Terminal officials put out a "hurry call" for shovelers to clear the railroad yards. The city's street cleaning department announced they were in need of an additional 150 laborers to shovel snow from the streets. Meanwhile, the refuse department directed all employees to work on shoveling and clearing the snow from streets before clearing trash.

To aid in the effort, 30 horses were teamed up with snow carts and were driven from the city's stables at Fourth and M Streets to the downtown business district to haul away the snow.

Five years after the disaster, Reggie Geare, the architect of the Knickerbocker Theater, found his career and reputation were ruined. Geare fell into depression and committed suicide in 1927. Ten years later, Harry Crandell, owner of the Knickerbocker Theater fell on hard times and turned the gas on in his apartment and committed suicide. Crandell left a note that explained, "I'm despondent and miss my theaters, oh so much." It was a tragic conclusion to an already tragic storyline.

The Ambassador Theater was built on the site of the Knickerbocker Theater and opened in September 1923. The Ambassador Theater was torn down in 1969, and a bank currently occupies the location.

WALTER REED HOSPITAL
WHERE SOME OF THE INJURED
FROM THEATER DISASTER WERE TREATED

This photograph of the Walter Reed Army Medical Center was taken after the Knickerbocker Snowstorm. A handwritten caption reads, "Walter Reed Hospital where some of the injured from theater disaster were treated." Many ambulances and members of the Walter Reed nursing staff were sent to the Knickerbocker Theater to help with the rescue effort. Later, family and friends of the victims and survivors had the challenging task of trying to locate their loved ones at the various hospitals in the area, including Walter Reed, or in the morgue. (The Historical Society of Washington, DC.)

A funeral for Knickerbocker Theater orchestra member Joseph Beal took place on February 4, 1922. There were many funerals in Washington in the days that followed the Knickerbocker tragedy. A total of 98 people were killed in the disaster. The dead were buried in many Washington-area cemeteries, including Congressional, Mount Olivet, Glenwood, and Arlington National Cemetery. At least 12 of the victims were from out of town, and funerals and burials occurred outside of Washington. A 17-year-old boy, David Lyman, who was killed in the Knickerbocker Theater, was buried at Congressional Cemetery (see page 79). Joseph Beal was buried at Arlington National Cemetery. (Library of Congress.)

These photographs show the Capitol after the Knickerbocker Snowstorm. After the snowstorm, horses pulling snow carts helped haul away the snow that was shoveled off the many walks and steps that surround and lead up to the Capitol building. The snow removal effort occurred in earnest for several days following the storm. The snow did not completely melt from the ground until February 10. (Library of Congress and The Historical Society of Washington, DC.)

The Washington Monument is pictured in the snow during the early 1920s, possibly after the Knickerbocker Snowstorm. The Washington Monument is a timeless landmark in 20th-century photographs. The 555.5-foot (169.3-meter) marble and granite obelisk defines the Washington skyline on the east end of the Reflecting Pool. The Washington Monument was completed in December 1884. (Library of Congress.)

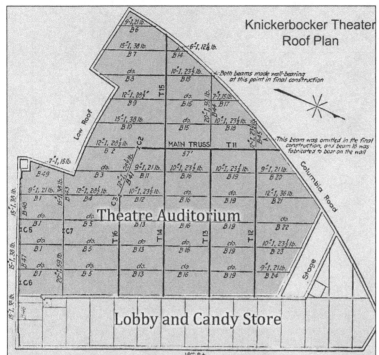

**Knickerbocker Theater Roof Plan**

Theatre Auditorium

Lobby and Candy Store

This illustration shows the theater's roof plan. The area labeled auditorium was the scene of the roof collapse and the location where most of the moviegoers were killed. The roof over the lobby and candy store did not collapse.

The publisher of *Washington News* commissioned this painting, *Knickerbocker Theatre Disaster*, by 24-year-old Rico Tomaso soon after the storm. The painting, a 26-inch-by-46-inch oil on canvas that shows the inside of the Knickerbocker Theater during the rescue effort, is part of the Georgetown University Library Special Collections Research Center. (Georgetown University Art Collection, Washington, DC.)

The Knickerbocker Theater was not the only structure to collapse during the snowstorm. A freight shed at First Street and Florida Avenue collapsed under the weight of the record-breaking snow. No one was inside the shed during the collapse. These photographs, taken February 1, 1922, show the 400-foot structure. Almost 90 years later, the Snowmageddon storm of 2010 would provide similar snowfall totals across the Washington area, and it would also collapse a few roofs, but not with the same deadly consequences as the Knickerbocker Snowstorm. (Both, Library of Congress.)

Schoolchildren are employed to help clear the streets from snow after the Knickerbocker Snowstorm. Hundreds of people were employed by the city for snow removal. Horse-drawn snow wagons were used to haul away the snow. (Library of Congress.)

US senator Ralph Cameron of Arizona shovels snow after the Knickerbocker Snowstorm on January 30, 1922. Cameron is best known for opposing the Grand Canyon becoming a national park. He suggested hydroelectric dams and a platinum mine be built on the land. (Library of Congress.)

After the Knickerbocker Snowstorm, the district's street cleaning department needed an additional 150 laborers to shovel snow from the streets. This early-1920s photograph could be of the Knickerbocker Snowstorm. (Library of Congress.)

The district's refuse department directed all employees to work on shoveling and clearing the snow. Thirty horses were teamed up with snow carts and snowplows. This early-1920s photograph could be of the Knickerbocker Snowstorm. The snow was shoveled into snow carts and dumped off the city streets. (Library of Congress.)

President Harding and his secretary, George Christian, inspect the snow removal efforts on the streets of Washington on February 3, 1922. Harding said after the storm, "The terrible tragedy, staged in the midst of a great storm, has deeply depressed all of us and left us wondering about the revolving fates." (Library of Congress.)

President Harding and George Christian walk the city streets inspecting the road conditions after the Knickerbocker Snowstorm on February 3, 1922. Mild temperatures followed the storm, which helped melt the snow from the city's streets. The road conditions during the inspection were fairly good. (Library of Congress.)

Senators Ralph Cameron, Arthur Capper, and Edgar Borah walk through the deep snow after the Knickerbocker Snowstorm on January 30, 1922. The house and senate, led by Senator Capper, called for a sweeping inquiry into the inspection and enforcement of building codes and practices across the District of Columbia. (Library of Congress.)

Gov. Scott Cordelle Bone of Alaska walks through the deep snow after the Knickerbocker Snowstorm. Bone was appointed by President Harding in 1921. He is best known for making the decision to use dog sleds to transport diphtheria antitoxin during the 1925 Serum Run, which later led to the annual long-distance Iditarod Trail Dog Race. (Library of Congress.)

Pictured is a volleyball game in the snow on February 1, 1922, at Bolling Field. Bolling Field was located in Anacostia on the east side of the Potomac River. In the 1940s, Bolling Field became Naval Air Station Anacostia, and Bolling Air Force Base was constructed nearby. Judging by the snow cover in this photograph, the game was only played for a few minutes. A warming trend

followed the Knickerbocker Snowstorm, and by February 2, the temperature reached 56 degrees. The temperature during this volleyball game reached 42 degrees during the afternoon. The snow melted quickly in the days that followed the Knickerbocker Snowstorm, and by February 10, 1922, almost all of the snow in the Washington area had melted. (Library of Congress.)

Secretary of the Navy Edwin Denby leaves a cabinet meeting in Washington and walks through snow-covered sidewalks after the Knickerbocker Snowstorm on January 31, 1922. Secretary Denby is best known for his part in assigning US Marines to protect the US mail from a rash of robberies in 1921. (Library of Congress.)

Secretary of the Interior Albert Fall leaves a cabinet meeting in Washington and walks through snow-covered sidewalks after the Knickerbocker Snowstorm on January 31, 1922. Secretary Fall is best known for his role in the Teapot Dome Scandal, which ultimately led to his resignation and jail time in 1924. (Library of Congress.)

Pictured at right is the inside of the Knickerbocker Theater during the clean-up effort on January 30, 1922. The outside walls of the Knickerbocker Theater were left in place and used with the construction of the Ambassador Theater, which was built on the same site the following year. (Library of Congress.)

Pictured below is deep snow near Lafayette Park on January 30, 1922. Lafayette Park is located directly across from the White House on Pennsylvania Avenue. The city of Washington, DC, was already well dug out from the snowstorm on January 30. (Library of Congress.)

Sir Paul Dukes poses in the snow after the Knickerbocker Snowstorm on January 30, 1922. Paul Dukes is best known as the "Man of a Hundred Faces" and is the only person knighted for his success in espionage. (Library of Congress.)

Pictured is a Lincoln impersonator on the White House lawn on February 9, 1922. Ten days after the Knickerbocker Snowstorm, most of the snow was melted. The official snow depth on February 9 was one inch. (Library of Congress.)

Pictured is the grave of David Lyman Jr., who was only 17 when he was killed in the Knickerbocker Theater. The grave site is at Congressional Cemetery. David's father died a year later of tuberculosis and is buried next to him. A lawsuit was brought against the Knickerbocker Theater Company by the estate of David Lyman. The family lost its case and appeal.

This is a photograph of the Knickerbocker Theater jury on February 15, 1922. Investigations were conducted by Congress, the city coroner, and the courts. The investigations concluded that faulty design and construction was responsible for the collapse. However, the courts were unable to determine who was liable. (Library of Congress.)

This is a Capitol snow scene after the Blizzard of 1888. A station attendant has cleared an area next to the tracks to allow passengers to board Washington's horse-drawn streetcars. The blizzard produced strong winds that knocked down thousands of telegraph wires in the area, cutting off all communication into and out of the city. Snowfall totals ranged from 2 to 10 inches, with accumulations heaviest to the north and west of Washington. Much less snow fell than during the Knickerbocker Snowstorm, but far more damage to the entire area was caused by the wind. (Library of Congress.)

# Five

# COMPARING STORMS

Situated between the Blue Ridge Mountains to the west and the Chesapeake Bay and Atlantic Ocean to the east, the Washington area is located in a classic "meteorological battle zone" during winter. The battle pits dry, Arctic air, which plunges south out of Canada, against relatively warm, moist air that streams in from the Atlantic Ocean and the Gulf of Mexico. The result often fuels big storms that dump heavy rain, snow, sleet, and freezing rain across the area.

For the Washington area to get a long-duration snow event, like that of the Knickerbocker Snowstorm, a lot of meteorological ingredients must come together, and stay together, for the duration of the storm. It is usually necessary to have cold high pressure anchored to the north and a slow-moving storm system tracking to the south and east. In addition, a good supply of moisture from the Atlantic Ocean and/or Gulf of Mexico must interact with the cold air. When all of the right ingredients come together, and stay together, a Washington, DC, snowstorm can be truly impressive and can rival any snowstorm of a northern US city.

On average, Washington receives one big snowstorm every 10 years. Some decades have few heavy snowstorms, while other decades can have multiple historic snowstorms in the same season, as was the case with the winter of 2009–2010.

Snowstorms that rival the Knickerbocker Snowstorm in Washington are quite rare. Since official records began, the list of rivals is short, including the Blizzard of 1983, the Blizzard of 1996, the Presidents' Day Snowstorm of 2003, and Snowmageddon 2010. None of these storms equal the Knickerbocker's snow total of 28 inches in Washington, but the storms did produce equivalent snow totals north and west of town. Snowmageddon 2010 even produced a 32.4-inch snow total at nearby Washington Dulles Airport.

There may never be a truly accurate comparison to the Knickerbocker Snowstorm because the city's measuring location was moved from the hills of northwest Washington at Twenty-fourth and M Streets NW down to Washington Reagan National Airport, which is located next to the Potomac River, at near sea level. The differences in elevation and the location's microclimates influence the snow accumulation, as has been noted with storms in the past.

George Washington and his Continental Army crossed the ice-clogged Delaware River on Christmas night of 1776 in a snowstorm. Washington and his army were en route to Trenton, New Jersey, to attack Hessian forces. One foot of snow and sleet fell in Trenton, and two feet of snow fell from Northern Virginia to central Maryland. (Library of Congress.)

This common sleigh scene is from the 1850s. On January 18, 1857, a severe snowstorm swept up the East Coast, dropping over 18 inches of snow from North Carolina to New England. Near-zero-degree temperatures ensured that the precipitation stayed mainly snow, even along the coast of southeast Virginia. Washington received 24 inches of snow. (Library of Congress.)

On December 26, 1890, ten inches of snow fell in Washington. It is rare for double-digit snowfall accumulations to occur in December in Washington. The December that preceded the Knickerbocker Snowstorm did produce a 4.5-inch snow accumulation.

Pictured is a snowdrift on H Street, across from the Government Printing Office, after the Blizzard of 1899. Snow fell in Washington for 51 hours, from February 11 to February 14, accumulating 20 inches. A series of snowstorms dropped 34.9 inches of snow in Washington and was accompanied by very cold temperatures and strong winds. Washington's all-time record low of negative 15 degrees occurred the day before the blizzard on February 11, 1899. (Copyright *Washington Post*; courtesy the District of Columbia Public Library.)

The band plays for President-elect Taft's inauguration. A surprise snowstorm dropped almost a foot of heavy, wet snow on the city on March 4, 1909. Due to the weather, President Taft moved the planned outside oath of office ceremony to inside the senate chamber. (Library of Congress.)

President Roosevelt and President-elect Taft ride inside a horse-drawn carriage en route to Taft's inauguration on March 4, 1909. Taft joked after the surprise snowstorm, "I always knew it would be a cold day in hell when I became President." (Library of Congress.)

Pictured is a horse-drawn sleigh with riders in front of the Lincoln Memorial. Horse and sleigh rides around Washington were a recreational and fashionable form of transportation during the 19th and early 20th centuries. Pennsylvania Avenue, Rock Creek Park, and roads around the monuments were favorite destinations for sharply dressed Washingtonians to go on old-fashioned sleigh rides. Sleigh riding, of course, was never a common form of transportation in Washington during the winter months due to the lack of consistent snow cover. For this scene, a snowstorm on February 4–6, 1920, dropped 6.5 inches of snow on Washington. The temperature never rose above freezing on February 5, which provided excellent conditions for sleigh riding. (Library of Congress.)

Kids clear snow off the ice on Rock Creek. A major cold outbreak occurred in the middle of January 1918. It was similar to the cold outbreak before the Knickerbocker Snowstorm, slightly colder, and it was followed by big snow that accumulated 14 inches over four days. (Library of Congress.)

A man pulls a small sled on the ice of the Reflecting Pool. The Reflecting Pool was a common destination for ice-skating in Washington. This photograph was taken during a cold outbreak in about the same time period as the Knickerbocker Snowstorm. (Library of Congress.)

Washington streets are pictured during the cold and snowy January in 1918. Over 20 inches of snow fell during the month. January 1918 is the all-time coldest month on record in Washington, with an average temperature of 23.6 degrees. The high temperatures that month were mostly in the 20s and 30s. The coldest temperature was one degree, and the warmest temperature was 50 degrees. Snow covered the ground in all but seven days that month. (Both, Library of Congress.)

Ice blocks, associated with a massive ice floe on the Potomac River, push into Dempsey's Boathouse and the Washington Canoe Club on February 17, 1918. The moving ice, piled 10 feet high, crushed two buildings after the winter's first thaw created a huge break up of ice on the Potomac River. Very cold and snowy weather preceded the thaw, resulting in very thick ice on the river. Farther down the Potomac River from Georgetown, where tides pushed against the ice floe, a huge ice ridge formed and grew upward in the middle of the river. During the thaw, temperatures warmed into the low 60s on February 12 and 15. This photograph was taken from the Aqueduct Bridge near Georgetown. (Library of Congress.)

A Texaco service attendant is ready to pump gas after the Knickerbocker Snowstorm. This photo was taken on January 30, 1922 and shows Frank Carlin's Alexandria Auto Supply which was located at 104 South Washington Street. (Alexandria Library Special Collections.)

Transportation was made difficult during the Knickerbocker Snowstorm on January 28, 1922. (Library of Congress.)

Senate pages have a snowball fight near the Capitol on January 2, 1925. A major snowstorm produced eight-inch snow accumulations in Washington over a two-day period. Several different snowball fights involving senate pages were photographed during this time period. (Library of Congress.)

This is a line for a New Year's Day reception at the White House on January 1, 1925. A snowstorm produced eight inches of snow January 1–2, 1925, with subfreezing temperatures. (Library of Congress.)

The first snowstorm of the 1938–1939 winter season in Washington occurred on November 25. The storm dropped eight inches of snow on the city with a high temperature of 34 degrees and a low temperature of 21 degrees. Pictured is a scene at the White House. (Library of Congress.)

Pictured is a horse and sleigh in Rock Creek Park on January 24, 1935. DC police closed 20 blocks for sledding and sleigh riding after the storm. Over 20 inches of snow fell in January 1935 in Washington. (Copyright *Washington Post*; courtesy the District of Columbia Public Library.)

This is a street scene facing Lafayette Park on February 7, 1936. A snowstorm dropped 14.4 inches of snow in Washington with temperatures that hovered in the upper teens. The heaviest snow fell to the southeast of the District of Columbia, with 18 inches of snow recorded in southern Maryland. (Copyright *Washington Post*; courtesy the District of Columbia Public Library.)

The Potomac River is frozen on February 8, 1936. The Weather Bureau reported that the river had its worst ice and snow conditions in many years. The snow cover on the ice ranged from 10 to 25 inches. (Copyright *Washington Post*; courtesy the District of Columbia Public Library.)

This person is struggling to make deliveries in the snow on March 29, 1942. Despite marginally cold temperatures and a high March sun angle, the snow fell hard enough to leave substantial accumulations on road surfaces. A wet snow blanketed the Washington area with 11.5 inches in town and up to 18 inches of snow in the northern and western suburbs. The high temperature was 35 degrees, and the low temperature was 32 degrees. (Library of Congress.)

Pictured is a snowball fight in the park on March 29, 1942. Heavy, wet snow accumulated 11.5 inches while temperatures hovered near the freezing point. (Copyright *Washington Post*; courtesy the District of Columbia Public Library.)

There were good sledding conditions on Capitol Hill on January 24, 1948. Snowfall measured 9.5 inches with a high temperature of 17 degrees and a low temperature of 10 degrees. (Copyright *Washington Post*; courtesy the District of Columbia Public Library.)

Kids sled in Upper Marlboro, Maryland, on November 6, 1953. The early-season snowstorm began as a tropical depression in the central Gulf of Mexico. (Copyright *Washington Post*; courtesy the District of Columbia Public Library.)

A police officer sands a road during an early-season snowstorm on November 6, 1953. The snowfall at National Airport was 6.7 inches. (Copyright *Washington Post*; courtesy the District of Columbia Public Library.)

This is a massive snowball in Upper Marlboro, Maryland, on November 7, 1953. An early season snowfall dropped 6.7 inches of snow on Washington while central Pennsylvania received as much as two feet of snow. (Copyright *Washington Post*; courtesy the District of Columbia Public Library.)

Movitave won Bowie's 1958 Miss Maryland Stakes in a blinding snowstorm on February 15, 1958. Washington received 14.4 inches of snow, which stranded many horse racing fans. (Copyright *Washington Post*; courtesy the District of Columbia Public Library.)

A car owner in the 400 block of Tenth Street evaluates the job of digging out on February 15, 1958. The snowstorm of 1958 produced very heavy snowfall rates, over three inches per hour. The snow accumulation at National Airport was 14.4 inches. (Copyright *Washington Post*; courtesy the District of Columbia Public Library.)

A gag photograph was set up by a George Washington University student in front of the White House on March 21, 1958. Heavy, wet snow accumulated 4.8 inches at National Airport, with temperatures slightly above freezing. Temperatures were slightly colder in the elevated areas just to the north and west of Washington, where over 20 inches of snow accumulated. (Copyright *Washington Post*; courtesy the District of Columbia Public Library.)

A pole was brought down by the weight of the snow on March 21, 1958. The precipitation began as rain but changed to heavy, wet snow, which accumulated 4.8 inches in Washington but ranged up to 33 inches in Mount Airy, Maryland. The liquid content of the rain and snow at National Airport was 3.75 inches. (Copyright *Washington Post*; courtesy the District of Columbia Public Library.)

A boy is walking home from school near Second and I Streets SE on January 13, 1964. During the previous day, 8.5 inches of snow fell in Washington, with a high temperature of 22 degrees and a low temperature of 18 degrees. (Copyright *Washington Post*; courtesy the District of Columbia Public Library.)

A snow cone cartop is pictured in Washington on February 3, 1961. Frigid, snowy weather gripped the DC area during the winter of 1961, with over 30 inches of snow measured at National Airport during the period from January 19 to February 12. (Copyright *Washington Post*; courtesy the District of Columbia Public Library.)

Hamilton Street in Hyattsville, Maryland, is pictured during the blizzard of January 30, 1966. The Blizzard of 1966 produced 13.8 inches of snow in Washington, with higher amounts to the south and east. The maximum gust during the storm was 54 miles per hour. (Copyright *Washington Post*; courtesy the District of Columbia Public Library.)

The WWDC helicopter rescues an expectant mother in Prince George's County after the Blizzard of 1966. Helicopters from the military, police, and radio stations teamed up for emergency rescue missions since snowdrifts blocked many area roads. One snowdrift on Route 1 near Washington measured 12 feet high. (Copyright *Washington Post*; courtesy the District of Columbia Public Library.)

Snow and cold dominated the month of January 1977. The low temperature in Washington was below freezing every day of the month. This is only the second month on record that this happened in Washington. (Copyright *Washington Post*; courtesy the District of Columbia Public Library.)

Ice-skaters enjoy perfect skating conditions on the Potomac River near the Fourteenth Street Bridge in January 1977, Washington's fifth coldest month on record with an average temperature of 25.4 degrees. (Copyright *Washington Post*; courtesy the District of Columbia Public Library.)

This photograph shows ice on the Chesapeake Bay at the Bay Bridge on January 1977. Ice interfered with boat traffic and oyster harvests. Ice breakers were needed. Few Middle Atlantic winters are cold enough to freeze over the Chesapeake Bay. A cold weather pattern became established in December 1976 and persisted through January 1977, freezing both the Potomac River and Chesapeake Bay. Late in January, headlines were made when Buffalo, New York, was hit by its worst blizzard on record. The Washington area was impacted by the cold temperatures and wind associated with the blizzard, but only snow flurries fell east of the mountains in the District of Columbia. (Copyright *Washington Post*; courtesy the District of Columbia Public Library.)

Pictured is Floral Street in Washington after the Presidents' Day Snowstorm on February 19, 1979. A very intense snowstorm hit Washington, starting on the afternoon of February 19, 1979, and lasting through the morning of February 20, 1979. The snowfall at National Airport measured 18.7 inches. The heaviest accumulations were to the east of the city, with 20 inches of snow falling in Baltimore, Maryland, and 22 inches falling in Upper Marlboro, Maryland. (Copyright *Washington Post*; courtesy the District of Columbia Public Library.)

An Alabama farmer uses his tractor to pull a car out of a snowbank near Capitol Hill on February 19, 1979. Farmers protesting on the Mall broke through police blockades and helped road crews and motorists around Washington after the President's Day Snowstorm of 1979. (Copyright *Washington Post*; courtesy the District of Columbia Public Library.)

An Air Florida passenger is being pulled from the icy Potomac River by a United States Park Police helicopter. The Air Florida Boeing 737 jet crashed into the Fourteenth Street Bridge and plunged into the Potomac River during a snowstorm on January 13, 1982. The storm produced six to eight inches of snow accumulation. The failure of the ground crew to properly clean ice and snow off the jet's wings was blamed as the cause of the crash. The death toll in the disaster was 78. Sixty years earlier, on January 28, 1922, the weight of snow collapsed the roof of the Knickerbocker Theater on hundreds of moviegoers. Two of Washington's worst disasters were caused by snowstorms. (Copyright *Washington Post*; courtesy the District of Columbia Public Library.)

The tail from Air Florida Flight 90 sits aboard a recovery raft on January 19, 1982. The jet only flew for about a mile before it stalled. A United States Park Police helicopter arrived minutes after the crash, and its crew lowered a life preserver on a rope and began to haul survivors to shore. The ensuing recovery effort was hampered by extremely cold weather, with temperatures plunging to negative five degrees on January 17, 1982. (Copyright *Washington Post*; courtesy the District of Columbia Public Library.)

Snow buries a neighborhood near Frederick, Maryland, on February 12, 1983. Frederick received 30 inches of snow. The maximum snow band associated with the storm stretched over Washington's western suburbs and extended west to the mountains. National Airport received 16.6 inches of snow; Manassas, Virginia, totaled 22 inches of snow; and Damascus, Maryland, measured 24 inches of snow. (Copyright *Washington Post*; courtesy the District of Columbia Public Library.)

Snow falls on Veterans' Day at the Vietnam Veterans Memorial in Washington, DC, on November 11, 1987. A snow of 11.5 inches fell at National Airport during the late morning and afternoon of November 11. There was a tremendous snowfall gradient associated with the storm; Washington's western suburbs received three to five inches of snow while eastern suburbs of Washington had up to 17 inches of snow. (AP/Wide World Photographs.)

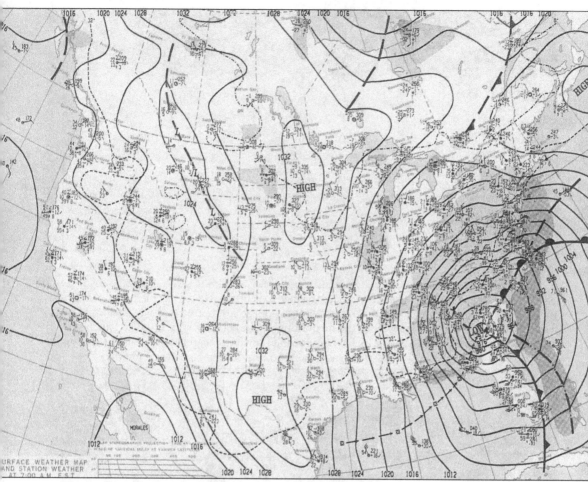

This is the surface weather map for March 13, 1993. The map shows the "superstorm" poised to move up the Eastern Seaboard. The Appalachian Mountains and interior regions of the eastern United States received the brunt of the snow, with two-foot accumulations fairly widespread from West Virginia to New York. To the south, Mountain City, Georgia, received two feet of snow, while Mount Mitchell, North Carolina, accumulated 50 inches of snow. In Washington, the snow turned to sleet and rain at the height of the storm, which greatly reduced snow accumulations. National Airport received 6.6 inches of snow with a 47-miles-per-hour wind gust. At Dulles Airport, 14.1 inches of snow fell, and at BWI Airport, 11.9 inches of snow fell. Record low pressures accompanied the storm. In extreme southwest Virginia, 30 to 42 inches of snow collapsed roofs. (NOAA Library.)

A man enjoys ski sailing by the Washington Monument on March 14, 1993. Six to 14 inches of snow fell across the Washington area on March 13. The snowfall at National Airport measured 6.6 inches, and the snowfall at Dulles Airport totaled 14.1 inches. The peak wind gust during the storm at National Airport clocked in at 47 miles per hour, from the northeast. Sleet and rain mixed with the snow in Washington, which reduced snowfall accumulations. Bitter cold temperatures followed the snowstorm and turned the soggy snow into a hard ice pack. At Snowshoe, West Virginia, the storm produced an amazing 54 inches of snowfall. All told, the storm was blamed for 200 deaths nationwide, and the total cost was estimated at $2 billion to repair damages. (AP/ Wide World Photographs.)

Pictured at left, there is very fast sledding down the Capitol steps on January 7, 1996. The storm dropped heavy snow from Washington to Boston. The snowfall at National Airport measured 17.1 inches, while the snowfall at Dulles accumulated 24.6 inches. Other snowfall totals included: 21 inches in Fredericksburg, Virginia; 22.5 inches in Baltimore, Maryland; and 25.7 inches in Rockville, Maryland. (AP/Wide World Photographs.)

Below, cars are buried in snow after the Blizzard of 1996 on January 8, 1996. Cold temperatures and two moderate snowfalls that followed the Blizzard of 1996 helped maintain a deep snow cover across the Washington area for more than a week. (Kevin Ambrose.)

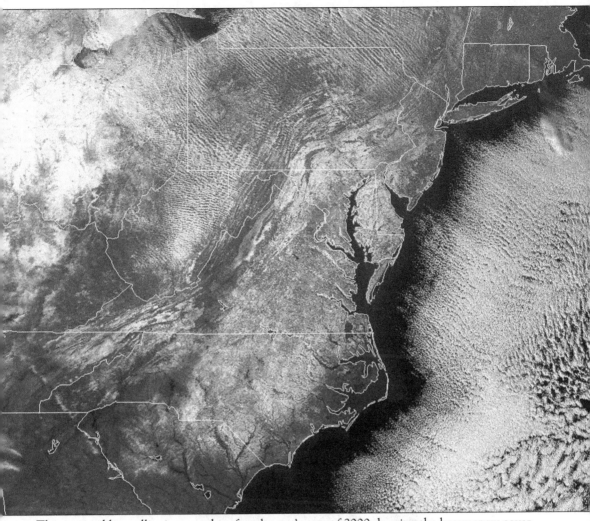

This is a visible satellite image a day after the nor'easter of 2000 showing the heavy snow cover over North Carolina, Maryland, and Virginia on January 26, 2000. New England was spared the worst of the storm while Raleigh, North Carolina, received 20 inches of snow. On January 24–25, an unexpected nor'easter hit North Carolina and Virginia. Between 8 to 18 inches of snow fell across the Washington area. The heaviest totals were to the east and south of Washington. The storm was a record-breaker in North Carolina. (NOAA Library.)

There are good cross-country skiing conditions on the National Mall on February 19, 2003. This photograph was taken near the Smithsonian Castle. The snowfall ranged from 15 to 28 inches across the Washington area. (Kevin Ambrose.)

Pictured is a snow tunnel after the snowstorm of February 18–19, 2003. The storm is also called the Presidents' Day II Snowstorm. This photograph was taken in Oakton, Virginia. (Kevin Ambrose.)

The sledding conditions were excellent during the snowstorm of February 11–12, 2006. The storm produced 8 to 32 inches of snow across a heavily populated swath from Northern Virginia through eastern Massachusetts. In the immediate Washington area, snowfall depths ranged from 8 to 17 inches, with increased amounts to the north and much less snow in central Virginia and southern Maryland. Near Columbia, Maryland, 21 inches of snow was reported. The storm achieved blizzard status in New York and New England as it rapidly intensified (bombed) to the east of Washington and moved up the East Coast. The low pressure became so deep that an eye formed and became visible on satellite images. At Reagan National Airport, 8.8 inches of snow fell during the storm, and 13.6 inches of snow fell during the entire 2005–2006 season, which is slightly lower than Washington's seasonal average of 15.6 inches. (Kevin Ambrose.)

Pictured is someone carrying groceries after the snowstorm of December 18–19, 2009. The snow total at Washington was 16.4 inches. Amounts ranged up to 22 inches or slightly more. The storm track was similar to the Knickerbocker Snowstorm. (Ian Livingston.)

This is a snow-blowing scene after the snowstorm of December 18–19, 2009. This storm was also named "Snowpocalypse" by the *Washington Post* Capital Weather Gang. This storm holds the record for Washington's greatest December snowstorm. (Ian Livingston.)

The Capitol Christmas tree is pictured on December 18, 2009. A storm the caliber of December 18–19, 2009, easily equals or surpasses an entire average snow for a winter season in the District of Columbia in a matter of one or two days. What became the biggest snowstorm since 2003 made it into Washington's top 10 snowstorm list, setting a new December standard. The 16.4 inches of snow that fell in the storm provided Washington snow cover until Christmas Day, when temperatures rose into the 40s and heavy rain quickly melted much of the snow. An even larger snowstorm would follow on February 6, 2010. (Jim Walline.)

Mount Vernon is photographed with deep snow cover on Christmas Eve of 2009. The 2009–2010 winter season was highlighted by historic snowfalls in late December and early February, which broke all-time records for monthly and seasonal snow totals. The federal government was closed for almost a week during the winter and both Virginia and Maryland declared states of emergency on multiple occasions. Mount Vernon and the entire Washington area had a white Christmas in 2009. In Washington, only 13 years in recorded history have had one inch or more of snow on Christmas Day since weather records began in 1871. These numbers indicate that the odds of a white Christmas in Washington are less than 10 percent. (Kevin Ambrose.)

The Marine Corps Memorial is photographed under a heavy blanket snow on February 7, 2010. Washington Reagan National Airport received 17.8 inches while nearby Washington Dulles Airport received 32.4 inches of snow. In late January 2010, the storm track in the eastern United States became quite active. From January 30 to February 10, four snowstorms dropped 30–60 inches of snow across the region. The snowstorm that occurred on February 5–6 was the largest of the 2009–2010 winter season and was named "Snowmageddon" by the *Washington Post* Capital Weather Gang. The snow was particularly heavy and dense, which caused widespread tree damage and a few collapsed roofs in the Washington area. (The United States Park Police.)

It is hard to tell where snow ends and the Chevrolet Suburban begins following Snowmageddon on February 7, 2010. Despite the heavy snowfall, the Knickerbocker Snowstorm record of 28 inches in Washington was still preserved. Using cars and people as benchmarks, the snow depths appear comparable with the Knickerbocker Snowstorm. (Kevin Ambrose.)

Cars are buried in snow in Cleveland Park after another snowstorm on February 10 dropped 10.8 inches of snow on Washington. This storm was named "Snoverkill" by the *Washington Post* Capital Weather Gang. The snow cover in Washington after this storm was well over 20 inches. (Ian Livingston.)

This beautiful Capitol snow scene was taken during Snowmageddon on February 6, 2010. Many considered it a "Storm for the Ages." Not only was the snow especially deep, mostly in the 20-inch to 30-inch range, but it was also very dense and heavy, which created widespread tree damage and power outages. (Ian Livingston.)

It takes a heavy, wet snow to accumulate inside of a basketball hoop. After Snowmageddon, this hoop is not only filled with snow, but it accumulates well above the rim. (Kevin Ambrose.)

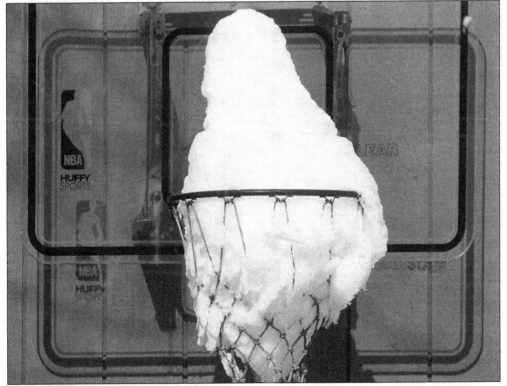

This is a view of the Jefferson Memorial and Tidal Basin after Snowmageddon on February 7, 2010. A United States Park Police helicopter was used to take photographs of the snow from above. (The United States Park Police.)

Below is a beautiful view of Great Falls and the Potomac River with snow plastered to the trees and rocks that surround the river on February 7, 2010. Over 25 inches of snow fell on Great Falls and Northern Virginia, and this storm does rival the Knickerbocker Snowstorm for snow depth, particularly just north and west of the city. (The United States Park Police.)

Blizzard conditions were severe in Washington on February 10, 2010. The snowstorm on February 10 produced snowfall in the range of 7 to 27 inches, with the least amount of snow occurring south of Washington and the greatest snowfall depth occurring north of the city, in northeastern Maryland. Washington was shut down on February 10 as road crews struggled to clear the roads. The storm began as wet snow, sleet, and freezing rain in Washington but quickly transitioned to a dry, drifting snow. Unlike with the Knickerbocker Snowstorm, which was massive dump of snow, the multiple storms of January and February 2010 provided a longer-lasting snow cover and many more challenges for snow removal. (Ian Livingston.)

**Washington's Top 10 Snowstorms on Record**

Storm snow total (in inches)

- 28.0 — 1/27-28/1922
- 20.5 — 2/11-13/1899
- 18.7 — 2/18-19/1979
- 17.8 — 2/5-6/2010
- 17.1 — 1/6-8/1996
- 16.7 — 2/15-18/2003
- 16.6 — 2/11-12/1983
- 16.4 — 12/18-19/2009
- 14.4 — 2/7/1936
- 14.4 — 2/15-16/1958

This chart shows the top 10 snowstorms for Washington, DC. The Knickerbocker Snowstorm is no. 1 with 28 inches of snow; the no. 2 snowstorm for Washington is the Blizzard of 1899 with 20.5 inches; and the no. 3 snowstorm is the Presidents' Day Snowstorm of 1979 with 18.7 inches. Snowmageddon 2010 is in fourth place with 17.8 inches of snow. (Ian Livingston and Kevin Ambrose.)

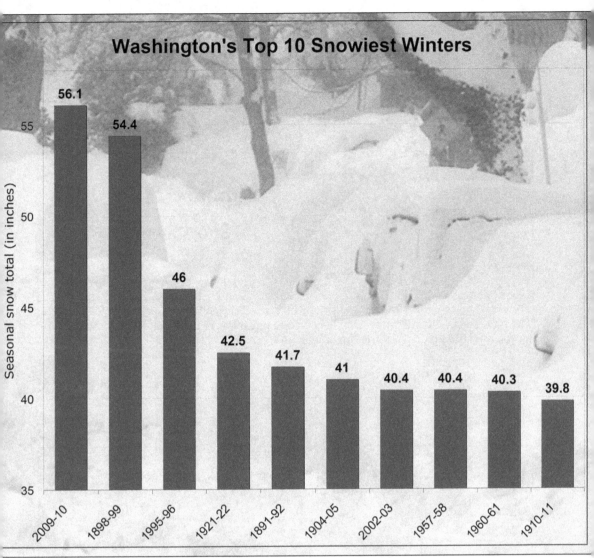

## Washington's Top 10 Snowiest Winters

Seasonal snow total (in inches)

| Winter | Total |
|--------|-------|
| 2009-10 | 56.1 |
| 1898-99 | 54.4 |
| 1995-96 | 46 |
| 1921-22 | 42.5 |
| 1891-92 | 41.7 |
| 1904-05 | 41 |
| 2002-03 | 40.4 |
| 1957-58 | 40.4 |
| 1960-61 | 40.3 |
| 1910-11 | 39.8 |

This chart shows the top 10 snowiest winters for Washington, DC. The winter of 1921–1922 is in fourth place for the snowiest winter. The winter of 1921–1922 featured one very large snowstorm, the Knickerbocker Snowstorm, and six small snowstorms that accumulated less than five inches each. It is interesting that the second largest snowstorm for the 1921–1922 season occurred December 4–5 and produced 4.5 inches. Weather historians will note that December 5 is a common date for the season's first snow in Washington. In comparison to the winter of 1921–1922, the no. 1 winter in Washington was 2009–2010, which produced two top 10 snowstorms and a third snowstorm that exceeded 10 inches. The winter of 2009–2010 is unprecedented in modern times, and it will take a very unusual winter to break that record. (Ian Livingston and Kevin Ambrose.)

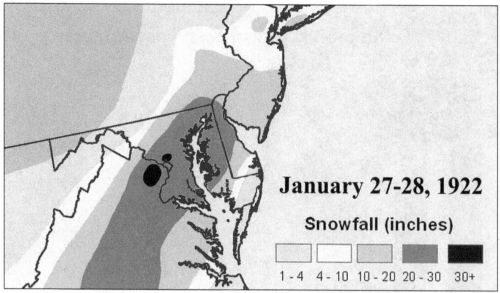

**January 27-28, 1922**

Snowfall (inches)

1 - 4   4 - 10   10 - 20   20 - 30   30+

The no. 1 Washington snowstorm was the Knickerbocker Snowstorm on January 27–28, 1922. The snow amount was 28 inches, the temperature range was 18 to 31 degrees, and the resulting snow cover lasted 15 days. (Kevin Ambrose.)

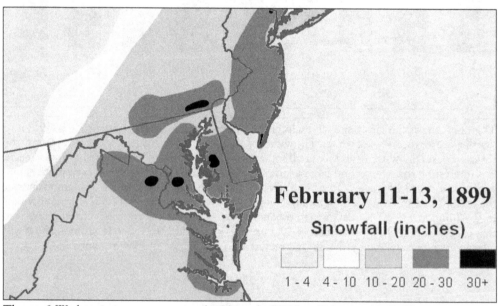

**February 11-13, 1899**

Snowfall (inches)

1 - 4   4 - 10   10 - 20   20 - 30   30+

The no. 2 Washington snowstorm was the Blizzard of 1899 on February 11–13. The snow amount was 20.5 inches, the temperature range was negative 15 to 12 degrees, and the resulting snow cover lasted 11 days. (Kevin Ambrose.)

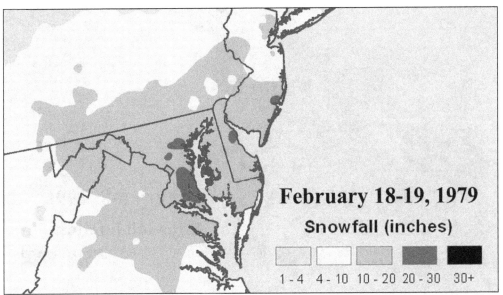

February 18-19, 1979

Snowfall (inches)

1 - 4   4 - 10   10 - 20   20 - 30   30+

The no. 3 Washington snowstorm was the President's Day Snowstorm on February 18–19, 1979. The snow amount was 18.7 inches, the temperature range was 6 to 36 degrees, and the resulting snow cover lasted eight days. (Kevin Ambrose.)

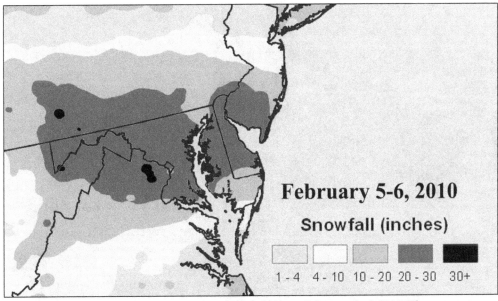

February 5-6, 2010

Snowfall (inches)

1 - 4   4 - 10   10 - 20   20 - 30   30+

The no. 4 Washington snowstorm was Snowmageddon on February 5–6, 2010. The snow amount was 17.8 inches, the temperature range was 21 to 37 degrees, and the resulting snow cover lasted 18 days. (Kevin Ambrose.)

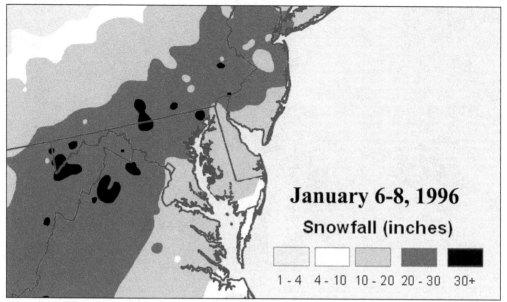

**January 6-8, 1996**

**Snowfall (inches)**

1 - 4  4 - 10  10 - 20  20 - 30  30+

The no. 5 Washington snowstorm was the Blizzard of 1996 on January 6–8. The snow amount was 17.1 inches, the temperature range was 18 to 30 degrees, and the resulting snow cover lasted 13 days. (Kevin Ambrose.)

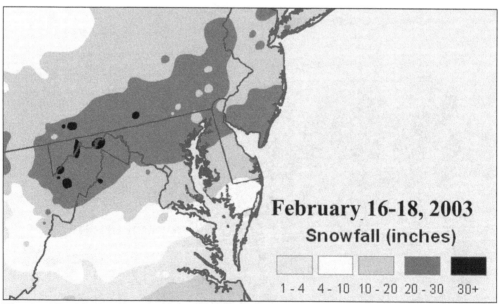

**February 16-18, 2003**

**Snowfall (inches)**

1 - 4  4 - 10  10 - 20  20 - 30  30+

The no. 6 Washington snowstorm was the President's Day Snowstorm II on February 16–18, 2003. The snow amount was 16.7 inches, the temperature range was 15 to 35 degrees, and the resulting snow cover lasted nine days. (Kevin Ambrose.)

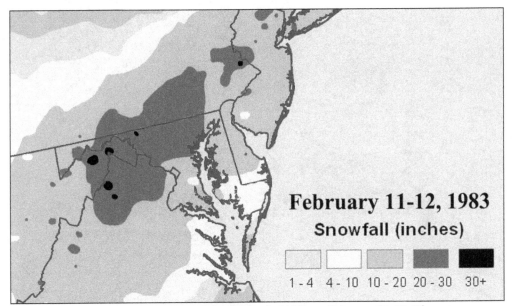

The no. 7 Washington snowstorm was the Blizzard of 1983 on February 11–12. The snow amount was 16.6 inches, the temperature range was 19 to 35 degrees, and the resulting snow cover lasted eight days. (Kevin Ambrose.)

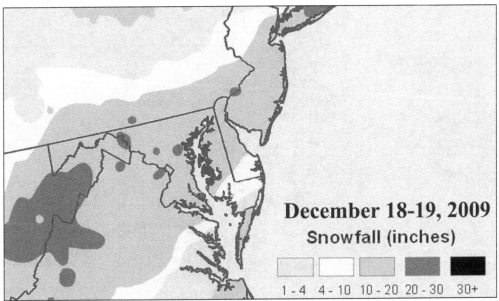

The no. 8 Washington Snowstorm was Snowpocalypse on December 18–19, 2009. The snow amount was 16.4 inches, the temperature range was 25–35 degrees, and the resulting snow cover lasted seven days. (Kevin Ambrose.)

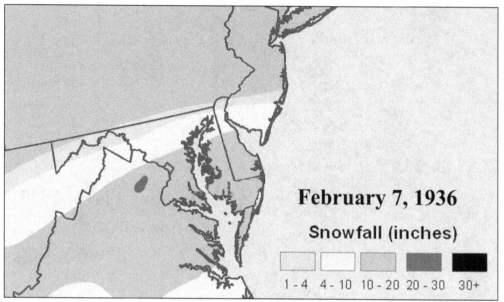

**February 7, 1936**

Snowfall (inches)

1 - 4  4 - 10  10 - 20  20 - 30  30+

The no. 9 Washington snowstorm was the Blizzard of 1936 on February 7, 1936. The snow amount was 14.4 inches, the temperature range was 16 to 25 degrees, and the resulting snow cover lasted 10 days. (Kevin Ambrose.)

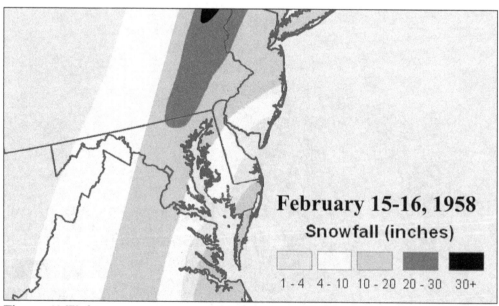

**February 15-16, 1958**

Snowfall (inches)

1 - 4  4 - 10  10 - 20  20 - 30  30+

The no. 10 Washington snowstorm was the snowstorm of 1958 on February 15–16. The snow amount was 14.4 inches, the temperature range was 11 to 32 degrees, and the resulting snow cover lasted eight days. (Kevin Ambrose.)

Pictured is the author with his first son, Bradley, after the Blizzard of 1996. The author has been interested in winter weather ever since he was in the second grade and realized that snowstorms cancelled Fairfax County Public Schools and created snow days and sledding opportunities for him and his friends. Ambrose majored in computer engineering at the University of Virginia but would sneak into meteorology classes during his free time. He wrote his first weather book, *Blizzards and Snowstorms of Washington, DC*, in 1993, and he currently writes for the *Washington Post* Capital Weather Gang blog. In addition to his interest in winter weather, Ambrose is interested in severe weather and storm chasing. He has photographed lightning striking the Washington Monument and has documented the destructive derecho of June 29, 2012, with photographs and video. Ambrose currently lives in Oakton, Virginia. (Elisa Ambrose.)

Visit us at
arcadiapublishing.com

CPSIA information can be obtained
at www.ICGtesting.com
Printed in the USA
LVHW062248310720
662073LV00001B/148

9 781531 666064